The Book of *Human* AWAKENING

A new understanding of everything we are and came here to be

Katie AND **THE CHORUS**

ISBN: 979-8-9852576-0-1, ebook
ISBN: 979-8-9852576-1-8, paperback

Cover Design and Typesetting:: HR Hegnauer, www.HRHegnauer.com
Cover and Interior Illustrations: Yev Mychak, www.YevMychak.com
Editing: Maggie McReynolds, Un-Settling Books, www.UnSettlingBooks.com

To all of you
From all of us

Table of Contents

Part 3

Introduction

This book came to me when I needed it. Likely, the same is true for you.

You've got questions, of course. I did too. Who is Katie? Who is The Chorus? What is this thing you're about to read?

I'll tell you some of it. But much like The Chorus themselves, I'll let the rest of it unfold for you as you go. It's too good to risk spoilers.

What I will tell you is that this is an introductory text, a magical story, a manifesto, a history, and a love letter. All those things, both alternately and all at once, and on some pages more obviously than others. It's what the title says it is: an invitation to wake up to all we agreed at one point to forget. And that, as it turns out, is a lot.

Many of us find ourselves ping ponging back and forth between going about our days as usual, bursting into brisk actions of hope, engaging in various means of overwhelmed distraction, and fending off a sort of muted existential despair. How did we get here? Is there a purpose, a point? Are we all as doomed as it sometimes seems? And is it even remotely possible that somehow everything could still turn out to be okay?

Okay, one spoiler. The answer to that last question is yes.

A book that purports to convey nothing less than humanity's origins and destiny could have been a pedantic slog. This is not that. The authors are patient, funny, personable, and loving. They are also, apparently, meticulous proofreaders. As a book editor, I don't think I've ever received a first draft manuscript as free from errors.

That's not to say there weren't things I got hung up on. I noticed that sometimes specific words were unexpectedly but not consistently capitalized. Sometimes numbers were spelled out and other times not. The vocabulary and style veered between casual and formal, even antiquated. I had to remind myself I was working with a *chorus* of authors. They may have spoken in unison – just as a musical chorus sings – but they were each harmonizing on a different note in the chord.

I grew to like these small reminders that they were all there. And while I was initially resistant to what felt like random capitalization and inconsistent numbering, I came to appreciate The Chorus's intentionality. If they unexpectedly capitalize a word, you can trust that they had a reason to do so.

I even came to find my own resistance interesting. I'd been digging in my heels at not just idiosyncratic grammar and punctuation but also over some of the concepts and ideas put forth in these pages. I noticed I was most resistant when I encountered the unexpected, or something I didn't quite understand. Sometimes I came up against something I wasn't sure I agreed with, and I'd find myself sort of arguing in the margin comments. "So what about …!?" I'd type. "Okay, but …" I'd write. "Something missing here???"

The answer was almost always something like, "Yes! That is a good question! More on this later!"

I am not the most patient of humans, and this was a little infuriating. How convenient, I thought, that the very thing I most want to know was something withheld, as if The Chorus were a cryptic Magic 8 ball.

It took me a while to get over myself. To set aside my ego, my need to *know* and be right. And, as time went on and my work with the manuscript deepened, I found my questions didn't seem as important, as urgent. I saw that many of my queries were playing "gotcha," as if I'd caught the authors out in an inconsistency or misstatement. I can be forgiven, perhaps, because this is what editors actually do. But there was something else going on too. I wanted whole-heartedly to believe The Chorus's message to humanity, and yet I was fighting with it. I was afraid, I realized, of being disappointed. I was arguing for my own limitations. And once I saw that, much of the energy I'd had for querulous inquiry began to dissipate.

This book is an immersive experience, and intentionally so. Like learning a language by spending time with those who speak it, as opposed to engaging in analytic, step-by-step instruction. When you're learning French, you don't ask why the "s" is silent or how come the letter U sounds tight. It just does – it's how it is. It's not necessary to know why in order to learn the language, even if there were a reason. In fact, drilling down into the whys can even be counter-productive. While you're busy demanding to know the sense behind irregular verbs, everyone else has learned how to ask for *croissants* and *chocolat* and is happily being fed.

The Chorus sees this book as the very beginning of an ongoing conversation. Where we humans want fast, even instantaneous, light-bulb moments, they invite us to simply stretch into these ideas and accept our perhaps only partial understanding. There is, in their view, no right or wrong way of doing anything, whether that's being a human or reading this book. We are, they assure us, right where we are supposed to be.

And so see if you can notice, without judgment, when you find yourself feeling resistant to any of the points they put forth. Resistance is, after all, a form of energetic engagement, and questions can just as easily be playful curiosity as opposed to angry challenge.

Do the examples given feel annoyingly vague? What if The Chorus had a reason for that? What if you didn't have to understand what that reason is?

Letting go of your what-about-isms and perceived need for microwave understanding allows you to relax into the authors' larger, broader perspective – like zooming out from Earth and seeing what a tiny and rather pretty blue planet we live on. Ahh. That's kind of a relief, in a world where everything feels urgent, desperate, frightening, on fire.

It's not necessary to resist your resistance. I didn't. I simply allowed it to exist but a little off to one side, resting on a comfy pillow. I could pick it back up any time I wanted to, but I didn't *have* to. I could just stay in the experience of reading the book.

I got so much more out of the book when I simply let it flow, and me along with it.

The message here is fascinating – and deeply reassuring. We – you – came here for a reason. All is unfolding as intended. There is no way to screw it up. We are, and have always been, more than okay.

I don't know about you, but that's a message I badly needed to hear right now.

So get a breath – get several – and settle in. You're about to go on a very joyful ride.

Maggie McReynolds, Editor
Boulder, Colorado, September 2021

The Book of *Human* AWAKENING

Before You Begin

Know that:

- You came here with specific purpose
- to experience limitation, which we call disallowance of energy, and
- by way of that disallowance, you would know, would experience, and would expand into your emotional array.

There are none who exist here, for any length of time, who did not gloriously, lovingly, and purposefully agree to these principles.

And simply by your existence here – no matter what you end up doing (or not doing), saying, building, creating, moving, or any of the many other words you have for "action" on your Earth plane – what you set out to accomplish is gloriously, lovingly, simply achieved.

This you must know first, for all other knowing stems from this simple fact. You wanted to be here. And by your being here, all you ever desired is achieved.

Know this: you are complete.

Kirby, [illegible]

You came here [illegible] specific purpose [illegible]

[illegible] to experience [illegible]

[illegible] and [illegible]

[illegible] way of [illegible]

[illegible] happens [illegible]

There are [illegible] length of time [illegible] did not [illegible]

[illegible] by your presence here [illegible]

[illegible] your Earth [illegible]

[illegible] simply [illegible]

[illegible] from this [illegible]

[illegible] complete.

Part 1

What You Have Been Experiencing

There have been five great epochs or eras of civilization in your history, spanning billions of your "years."

Through these epochs, you were able to experience – in radiant detail – vast regions of your emotional array, or as you call it today, your emotional spectrum. Each epoch, therefore, is characterized by a kind – a category – of *disallowance*, for in disallowing energy, you *feel* it. You call these feelings *emotions*. We call it your ability to perceive an *infinite* variety of ways to disallow energy. Let us explain.

Before you came "here," you existed in the pure flow of energy that is the source of all creation. In this pure flow, there is infinite love, energy, light, and life. All that you desire is instantly granted, in an endless flow of marvelous expansion.

In this pure stream of energy, you developed the desire to know parts of yourself more fully. These parts of you are able to demonstrate, to reflect, disallowance of energy.

Since disallowance is not the natural order of creation, in order to experience these things, you needed to create an environment in which to do so, where the rules of engagement could be different.

Out of pure love, you were given the energy to create this environment of disallowance. And you have been constantly creating it all these many years. For it is your desire that has energized this environment of disallowance. Without it, you would – and will – naturally, perfectly, and completely return to pure flow.

As you have surmised, your desire to experience limitation is evolving to the next step, a new step, on your path of greatest expansion. Which is why you, dear reader, are able to perceive this book today.

Chapter 1

What You Built

It is no small thing to create an environment that disallows the pure flow of all creation! Yet, you have done it. And as you continue to awaken to what you created, you will marvel at it all. This vast machine of disallowance, of limitation, is so complete and so powerful. There are many more than you can yet imagine who have enjoyed the opportunity to participate here.

One way to think about this environment is with the concept of the egg. Outside the egg is the pure flow of all energy. However, as energy hits the egg it is modified or molded into the creation of limitation. Therefore, it is important to remember that there is *not* limitation within the egg because of a *lack* of energy. That would be impossible. You cannot cut yourself off from what you are, which is energy (although that would be an interesting experience).

As much energy flows in here as in any other part of the universe. It is this energy that is used to create disallowance, limitation, and lack.

Your field of perception – of conscious awareness – has been limited to only those energies within the egg. Else it would ruin the experience. You cannot experience disallowance while being aware of pure flow! To you, in this perception, limitation was the way of all life, of creation. Your perception was perfectly constrained so that you would experience this environment to its fullest.

"What is the egg made out of?" you might wonder. What powerful construction re-shapes the energy of creation in an unbroken line of disallowance going back millennia?

It is your beliefs.

A vast matrix of intertwining, connected, and powerful beliefs that together filter the flow of energy into a very potent experience of the seeming lack of energy. Each belief was constructed, piece by piece, by every participant who ever shared these wavelengths.

If you took all the water, in all the oceans, in all the galaxies, from the deepest depths to the highest waves – and every single drop was a belief – it would still not come close to adequately describing the vastness of this matrix.

We call this amazing creation your Belief System Complex, or BSC.

This Belief System Complex (BSC) is fluid, dynamic, and ever evolving. Though from the inside, we understand that beliefs may seem static or slow-moving, in actuality the BSC is updated billions of times per second by every single participant who, by their energetic presence here, contribute to its creation.

A balance is always carefully struck between new energies flowing in and beliefs that constrain these things into the perception of limitation and lack. It is the combination of all life here that energizes this construction. You came here to play – you contributed your energy, while here, to maintaining the game field.

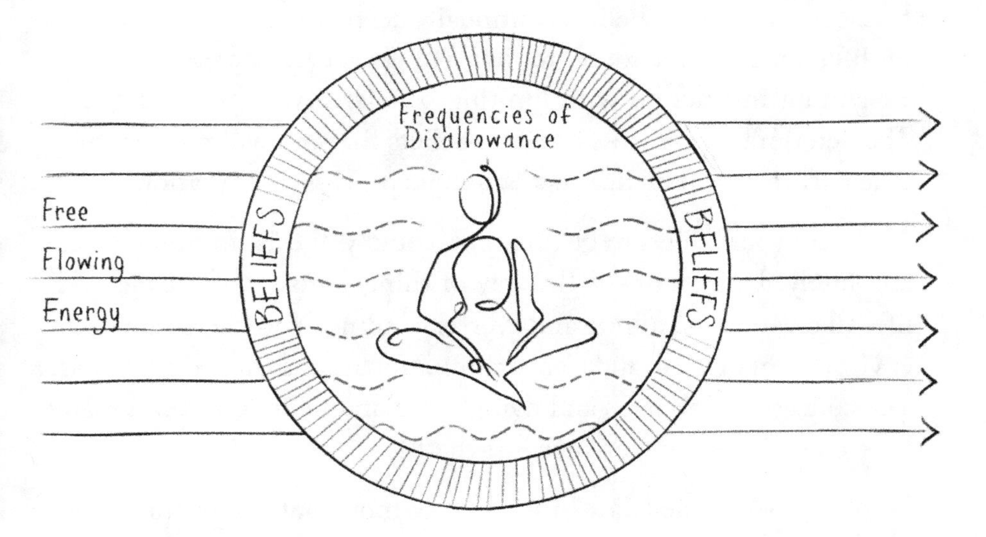

Illustration 1: The Concept of "The Egg"

You are, of course, unaware of your participation in the Belief System Complex (BSC). You do not name – consciously, billions of times per second – all the beliefs you have just created. Or that all the others have created, for that matter!

Rather your focus has been narrowed, by choice, to the game itself. To the experience of limitation and all the corresponding emotions you feel, second by second, day by day, all your life.

You are constantly being "birthed" into this Belief System Complex (BSC). From the moment of your arrival here, your connections to these beliefs continually deepen as you move forward in life, until you choose to depart. This ever-increasing, ever-expanding interaction with limiting beliefs is what you call aging. The deterioration process is due to beliefs that you willingly, joyfully take part in to experience such a unique process of limitation.

Were your beliefs to be different, could you exist infinitely? Yes, absolutely. In fact, this is the way of things outside of the egg. All life, all creation, is infinite and ever-expanding. You had to create an environment of profound lack, of limitation, to experience otherwise. The concepts of aging – and dying – are unique indeed. And many have come here to experience just that!

When someone "dies," they simply move outside of this Belief System Complex (BSC). From this vantage point, they may move on to any number of other experiences of their choosing, even coming back here. They can, and often do, vividly recall any aspect of their lifetime here that they wish. For nothing is ever lost in creation. To "lose," to "forget," are beliefs of *this* Belief System Complex (BSC). It is not the fundamental order of creation.

Thus, when someone dies, it is by your beliefs that you lose them – the ability to perceive them, the ability to interact with them, even, over time, the ability to remember them clearly. What a powerful experience of limitation! The idea that you could ever lose anything is a marvel to those of us outside of the egg. But that you could lose someone you love? Even more so! For it is concretely, absolutely impossible. Love is a powerful, unbreakable force – even here, inside the egg, where so much has been constructed to disallow, you still feel and are conscious of a force you call love. And here you are *so loved* that you have been given the power to create the perception, the experience, of loss.

What extraordinary emotions – that is, versions of disallowing energy – you experience by way of perceived loss of all kinds! You might lose your car keys, which feels like one kind of loss (even better to lose them when you are running late to something important!). You might lose something very precious to you, which feels like another way (even better if it is unique or ancient and completely "irreplaceable!"). You might lose a cherished pet, a dear friend, or a beloved family member to "death," which can feel, as you well know, bottomless and all-consuming. The weight can be difficult to bear.

So robust are your beliefs – so vast and unconscious – that even our bringing up these topics will cause you to resonate with this disallowance of energy. Some of you may have even consciously recognized a twinge, a pang, as these topics call to mind memories of the resonant experiences you have had in your lifetime.

But now, Beloved, you are so ready to expand beyond these frequencies that we are able to tell you why this is.

Chapter 2

What You Agreed To

Your path of greatest expansion led you here, to these particular frequencies of energetic disallowance. By your resonance with these frequencies, you created all the marvelous aspects of the Belief System Complex (BSC) and your physical experience of it.

When you resonate with a frequency, any frequency, you are agreeing with it. You are in alignment with it.

When you are ready to resonate with a different frequency, that "readiness" is actually a reflection that you have already begun to resonate with a new frequency, which is what you are doing here with us.

There is actually no dis-resonance or discordance. You do not first vibrate against a frequency you are on and break free of it. This concept of needing to push against is of *this* BSC.

In actuality, all creation is resonant, is attractive. Your frequency changes, and you are brought to the matching wavelengths effortlessly.

For us, outside the egg, this explanation is sufficient. You vibrated with these frequencies of limitation. But we understand now that, though you are transitioning, part of you still exists from the perception of conscious mind. Thus we will take this explanation a little closer to those frequencies, or places of understanding, so that the connection is built.

The Core Tenets

In vibrating with these frequencies, you agreed to everything that had been built, as well as to contribute to its continual construction.

We could describe to you everything that has been built – meaning, all of your beliefs – and it would only take a few million years. Unfortunately, by your beliefs, you would likely "expire" before we were done!

So to speed up the process, rather than describe each belief, we will convey the main, critical categories into which these beliefs fall. Please keep in mind that these things are fluid, evolving, and interconnected, so our simplification will draw artificial delineations between concepts. But for general description purposes, it should suffice.

It is finite

With each core tenet, or principle, of your Belief System Complex (BSC), you will notice a pattern: that it is backwards from the natural order of creation. This has caused an abundance of amusement for those outside your BSC, because the way humans think the universe works is very much the opposite of what it truly is! "How do they keep coming up with this stuff?!" is something many have said! We tease you, Beloved, because there is a part of you that has been in on the joke the whole time. It is only your mind-based consciousness that is reconnecting to this knowledge – for a part of you *had* to believe it in order to experience it.

This pattern of human beliefs running opposite to the flow of Creation has never been more true than in the first core tenet of this BSC, which is that creation is finite.

This vast collection of beliefs has remained largely unconscious until recent millennia. You did not often think to wonder why things were *not* infinite – they just were not. And your perceived physical environment gave you *consistent, thorough evidence of this.*

If you only see one pickle left in a jar, you are almost "out of" pickles. You'll have to do some physical things to get more.

The sun sets, there is no more daylight today. You'll have to wait until your planet turns around again to get more.

You see it everywhere, do you not? Stuff. Runs. Out. *If more doesn't come in*, you will run out of money, food, and energy. There is only so much metal in the ground. There is only so much water in the lake.

Even one of your fundamental laws of physics has stated this to be so. The Conservation of Matter says that through all changes, matter is neither created nor destroyed, based upon the assumption of a "closed system." And yet, it is only *very recently* that the idea has occurred to you that maybe the closed systems in your reality, which you thought you understood, may not quite yet be understood at all.

How interesting is it that, as you have begun vibrating toward new frequencies, you are able to see further into the space around your planet, but can't *quite see the end of it?*

It is not that this belief is being undone. It still holds true, powerfully true, for a great many who *are not done experiencing it*. But for you, it feels a little less true, a little less certain, than it did. And from time to time, you even stumble upon physically perceived evidence that calls into question the finiteness of what you consider reality.

It is not enough

Your beliefs about the finiteness of reality are so intertwined with your beliefs that there is often not *enough* that it is almost impossible to untangle them.

The concept of finiteness, alone, is vastly limiting compared to the infinite flow of energy you came from. But you took it a step further. You created beliefs that there was also not enough – or rather, *just barely* enough.

These vast empires of beliefs govern everything related to your perceived survival here. You believe these things so unconsciously, so concretely, that they define the majority of your lifetime.

Why is it that you cannot get everything done that you have ever desired in 1 day?

Why don't you hit all green lights everywhere you drive?

Why can't you eat food once and be satisfied for the year? Your lifetime? Eternity?

Why is the thing you were so excited about when you were six not equally exciting today?

These things feel absurd because of your participation in beliefs about insufficiency.

But of course, I can't eat food once and last forever. I must find more food.

But of course, I can't get excited once and feel that way for however long I wish. It fades. And then I look for other things that make me excited.

And thus, your participation in this reality was set. With a *limited supply* that can easily be *not enough*, the underlying game board for a great many experiences of limitation was established. And you, as a particular kind of human, added important beliefs to this setup that amplified further your experience of the disallowance, limitation, and lack.

The 3 Engines of Reality

The concept of reality is something that causes your kind a wide variety of emotions – that is, perceptions of disallowance – because it has been *so* limiting.

From our vantage point, reality is another term for perception of energies. Your reality is how you perceive and experience energy, our reality is how we do it. We find the most fun to be when you get to partake in how another perceives energy and see it all from their point of view, which is completely possible on energetic wavelengths.

But guess what you did here? You made it backwards. Not only are you completely unable to experience another's existence energetically but, until very recently, it did not even occur to you that there could be *any other way* to see the world than your own. (Recently, you are really beginning to awaken to the wide variety of realities out there, are you not? How much you discover on your social media!)

Thus reality was static and solid. You simply lived it. You disconnected yourself from all the beautiful, fluid, abundant ways of perceiving energy and locked yourselves into one – which could even span lifetimes. How unchanging! How beautifully, gloriously, completely limiting!

This was a great accomplishment indeed. To live in a reality – that is, a perception of energies – that views existence as finite and insufficient but then to also prevent yourselves from perceiving realities that would do it any other way. How did you do it?

You did it by way of additionally molding the energies you received via 3 marvelous regions of belief. Beliefs that were unprecedented unto the galaxies, and that have been the underlying driving forces of all of your experiences of limitation here.

Time

Again, we are delineating between things that are fluid and interconnected, but we think this one will make sense, as it is something that feels very concrete to you.

Time is, in a way, a culmination of your beliefs in finiteness and insufficiency. It governs, both consciously and unconsciously, every aspect of your physical experience of "reality" (which is how you perceive energy). *Everything* – every energy you receive – passes through the lens of time. It is a steady force, a steady presence, that applies, or embodies, the Core Tenets.

The "steady march of time," you call it. A good name for all the unconscious, vast oceans of belief that you have about time that consistently, relentlessly, create your reality.

You do not consciously make time pass. It just does. But consciously, you do deal with its effects, which are constant manifestations of lack and limitation. It structures everything you perceive. Even our earlier examples of finiteness and insufficiency make more sense to you when appended to the concept of time.

"Eat once and not be hungry for *2 years?* Absurd. I get hungry every *2 hours.*"

"Write an entire novel in 15 *minutes?* Ridiculous! No one could type and think that fast."

"Live to be *300 years old?* Not possible! How would you prevent all the inevitable deterioration?" (That is, as you now know, finiteness and insufficiency, enacted by your beliefs in the passage of time.)

You have strong beliefs about what can be possible in any given span of time. And everyone who shares these wavelengths agrees with these rules. You do not build an entire house in 1 hour, while it takes the "average person" eight months. You do not travel around the world in 5 seconds while it takes the rest of the people of your time several days. **There is always a general, evolving consensus about how long things should take, which manifests the limitation in every action you make.**

Beloved, time is not a fundamental part of creation. It is simply an element in this Belief System Complex (BSC).

THE "3 ENGINES" OF REALITY

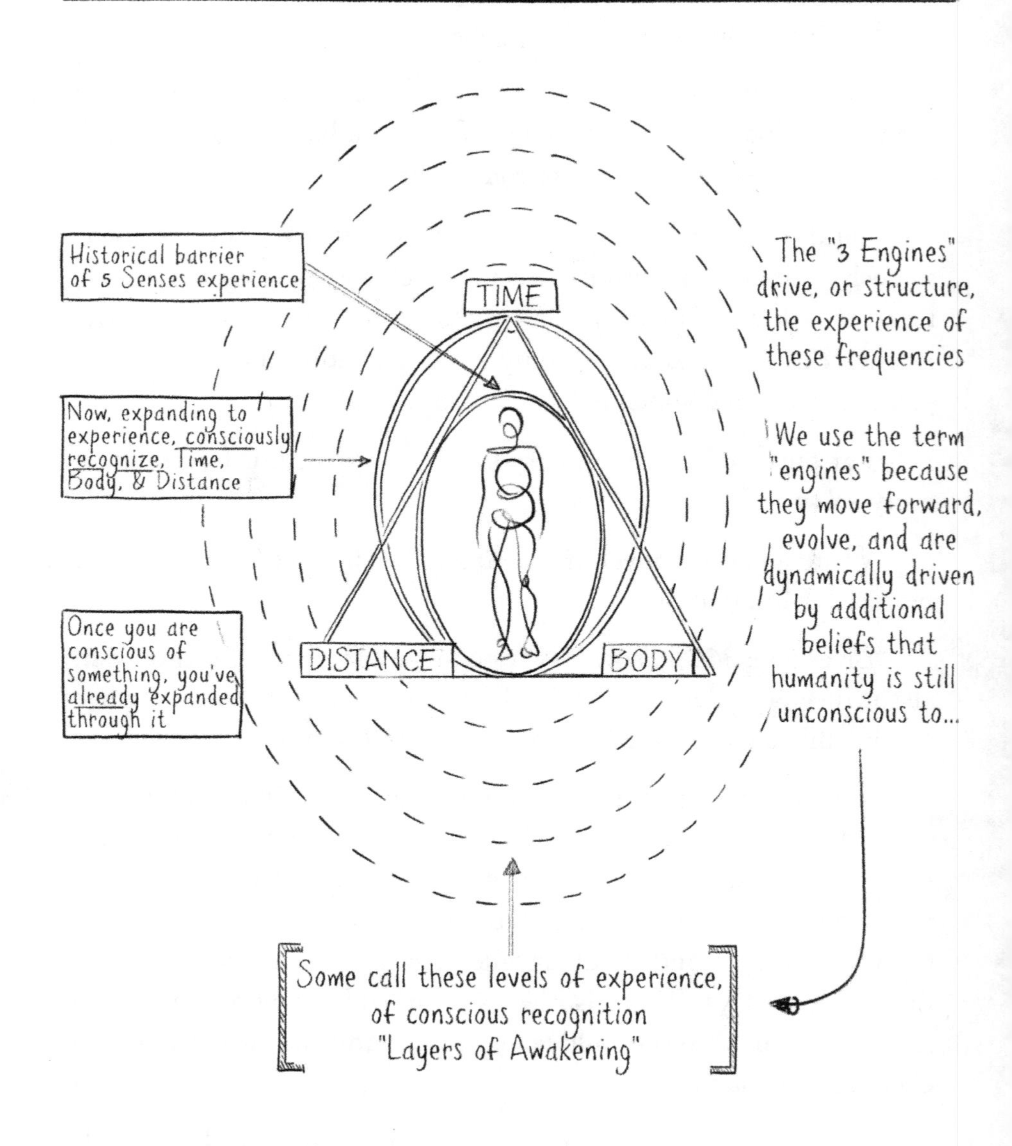

Historical barrier of 5 Senses experience
Now, expanding to experience, consciously recognize, Time, Body, & Distance
Once you are conscious of something, you've already expanded through it
TIME
DISTANCE
BODY
The "3 Engines" drive, or structure, the experience of these frequencies
We use the term "engines" because they move forward, evolve, and are dynamically driven by additional beliefs that humanity is still unconscious to...
Some call these levels of experience, of conscious recognition "Layers of Awakening"

Illustration 2: The "3 Engines" of Reality

As you vibrate toward new frequencies, you will discover the laws of time will soften, and the limitations time enacted will ease. Already a distance that used to take weeks or months to cross now takes only hours thanks to the manifestations of cars, trains, and planes. Knowledge that used to take years to find and uncover now arrives in minutes due to the manifestations of computers and the internet. These manifestations will only continue to grow, and you will enjoy the process, for it is on your path of greatest expansion.

Distance

Your beliefs about distance are quite closely intertwined with your beliefs about time. In fact, from certain vantage points, they make up a unified structure of the Belief System Complex (BSC).

"Distance" is what you have chosen to call your ability to perceive the difference between frequencies. What you might call different places, or "here" and there," are to us simply two different frequencies, which we might call frequency A1 and frequency A2, were we to put them in your language.

An important distinction, however, is that what we would view as the teensiest, tiniest difference between frequencies you view as literally miles apart. This manifestation – this conscious perception – about distance is due to how your beliefs in distance enact finiteness and insufficiency.

You only have so much energy in your body, and only so much time in your day, to get all the things done that you need to for your survival. Adding the need to *travel distances* to that list prompts further difficulties and challenges.

Moreover, when the desire to voyage distances has arisen in your history, the difficulties – the limitations – were so great that you often didn't get very far at all. You mostly stay on the same *frequency*, the same place, the majority of your lives. In a universe of infinite frequencies, full of infinite capacity to experience them all, you stay stuck on the same note!

Oh, our Beloved Ones, how you make us laugh. You perceive a great difference just between the city and the suburbs, between Phoenix and LA, between the Caribbean and the South Pole. And, in actuality, yes, these are different frequencies. Yet another, equally valid perspective is that you do not really change frequency until you leave your galaxy – and currently you just barely, consciously, get off your planet!

Do you see how specifically, how minutely, you have limited yourselves by way of your beliefs about distance? That there even *is* distance – meaning a gap that you must employ energy and time to get across?

If you can create beliefs that create disallowance billions of times per second, you are equally capable of changing frequencies – that is, locations – billions of times per second. So quickly that, viewed from a certain perspective, it might seem as though you could be "everywhere at once."

Do you see how recent manifestations bridge the gap so that others do not seem *so* very far away? Your relative may live in a distant country, but you can log on to a video call and see her instantly. This is closer to life outside the egg where, in pure flow, you could very easily vibrate to her location in a moment.

Body

The third engine of finiteness and limitation, intricately tied to time and distance, is the human body itself. What you view as a solid thing is actually a composite of very particular wavelengths that you take as one unified perception. These wavelengths are what you call your "five senses" – the wavelengths of sight, hearing, smell, touch, and taste. It is the way by which you view the world and also the way you do not view the world. For there are a great many things on a great many wavelengths that you do not yet perceive! You have begun to realize this in your sense of the electromagnetic spectrum – that there is infrared and ultraviolet, wavelengths that are real, and have effects on you, but are not readily perceived by the five senses.

Thus, what you perceive based on these wavelengths is vastly limited. And moreover, you agreed that the mind would make decisions, would take action, based upon the perception of these wavelengths alone. How limiting! How narrow! How specific! You have infinite capacity to know anything you ever desire, and yet you limit yourself to what you can see, or hear, or touch – and these in themselves are vastly reduced wavelengths of what is possible to be seen, heard, or touched.

As such, your experience of limitation was bound and complete. From the infinite flowing energy from which you come, you created an environment of finiteness and insufficiency further limited by concepts of time, distance, and the physical instrument you created to experience these wavelengths.

So much is ahead for you to discover, experience, and remember. So very much indeed.

Chapter 3

Why You Agreed to This

Just as you all agreed to abide by a similar conception of time and distance, so too did you agree to the general guidelines of what could be possible with your physical instrument, the body.

While some may run a little bit faster than the rest of you, or some may hear a little bit better than others, there are none who break the rules entirely who are still perceived by this Belief System Complex (BSC). Were you to jump off your roof and fly, or breathe deeply where there is no oxygen, you would have an enjoyable time, but you would – quite quickly – be evicted from participation in the BSC. Meaning, in some ways you would no longer be able to perceive this portion of the game field, and players on the field would not necessarily be able to perceive you. Bend the rules too far, and you're out of the game.

This is important to maintain the game for the remaining players. If, in the midst of their glorious struggling and toiling, they perceived a like member who could do everything with the snap of a finger, their beliefs in the *need* to struggle and toil would be fundamentally altered. Thus, they do not perceive it.

This is what has happened several times in your history with the ones who are considered "holy." Their abilities to bend the rules of your BSC had effects on the general consensus of the beliefs in the BSC that are still felt. Please know, however, that you all agreed to the experience of these exceptions as part of your gradual awakening. In the same way, you have allowed in the words that are here on these pages. This BSC is a consensus-driven experience.

Are these powers, these capabilities, completely possible? Of course. But they were not the objective of *this* game. Remember, you come from infinite flow. Having everything you wish is old news! What is novel, what is unprecedented, what is special and unique, is the experience of this limitation. And so much energy, so much participation, has gone into the creation of this marvelous egg.

This is exactly, perfectly, abundantly everything you desired. For, as we have stated, before your arrival here, you purely desired to know limitation. And to know the parts of yourself that reflect your ability to navigate limitation. These abilities are what you call your emotions.

You believe, consciously, that emotions are a feeling response to stimuli, both in your environment and mental activity. You have awakened to the fact – very recently in terms of the great epochs you have spent here – that the way you *think* about a thing can result in the way you *feel* about a thing. This is not untrue, from a conscious perspective. But now we would like to bring some new things to your consciousness.

All emotions that you feel in this physical reality are due to the vast Belief System Complex (BSC). Both consciously and unconsciously, billions of times per second, your limiting beliefs – which are the heart and soul of your consciousness here – cause disallowance of energy. The billions of ways in which this occurs are perceived by you emotionally. Humans are in a constant flow of changing emotions based on the ways they consistently, constantly, disallow energy throughout their entire existences here.

In recent epochs, you have become more aware of this ongoing emotional response, far more so than when you first arrived here. You now have a vocabulary for these things you feel. You now have professional healers who focus on the ways you feel. There are books on the topic, conversations on the topic, it is not even uncommon any longer to express – out loud, on the specific wavelengths of sound – how you feel.

See how far this has come for you. That what was once an entirely unconscious – and incalculably beneficial – aspect of your existence has recently become conscious. You are starting to receive it, to perceive it. "What *is* all this stuff we are feeling!?" many of you now wonder.

You push back against these emotions automatically, as is your programmed response of disallowance, even before you consciously recognize you are doing so. This energizes the emotions further – but we will get to that.

For now, understand that the Belief System Complex (BSC) is the vast, underlying structure that drives all of the emotions you feel, second by second, day by day, all of your conscious life. In some cases, your mind catches on to the thought that is driving your emotion and attempts to modify it, but in the majority of cases this is still running unconsciously behind the scenes, all the time.

In a way, it may feel like the Belief System Complex (BSC) is behind the wheel of your life, and you are an unwitting passenger. And in actuality, this is so! But let us take a broader view to discover why this is so, and why you gleefully, joyfully, revelrously agreed to this.

BELIEF SYSTEM COMPLEX ("BSC")

Mind, the Belief System Complex, perfectly limited the perception of all but a few energies used to instigate emotional response.

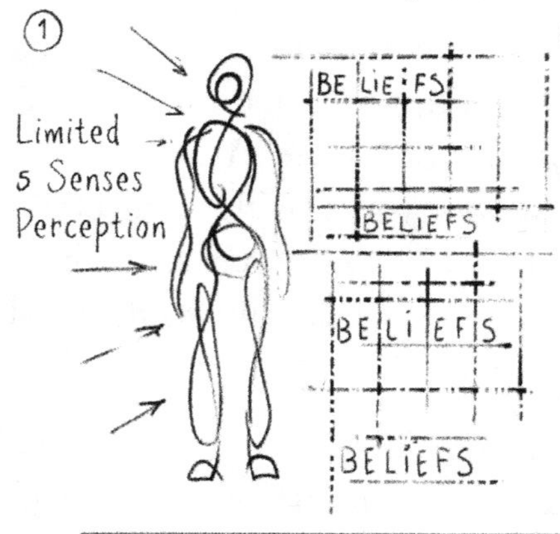

② Constantly activates the Belief System Complex

↳ which are REASONS to FEEL

{EMOTIONS}

over and over and over and over to great depth of familiarity

This happens billions of times per second. Or, said another way, TRIGGERS, fluidly, billions of points in the emotional array every second.

"But," you say, "I'm only aware of perhaps a few hundred emotions per day at most?"

YES, your awareness, intentionally, has been limited by mind's capacity so that you could be fully immersed in the experience.

You came to experience the unconscious drive through the emotional array, not to name everything in it with the 5 Senses.

TWO CONTEXTS FOR EMOTIONS

(1) Artificially triggered by the constructs of this environment (5 Senses Perception / BSC) where it is unconscious but experienced

(2) True abilities of your emotional array, which is to serve as a navigational compass across infinite wavelengths

All experiences remain with you, infinitely.
Though consciously (in mind's capacity) you do not recall all of these emotional experiences all at once, they are yours.

You created the perfect training ground (experiential field) to experience, in a powerful, condensed, complete way all that you are, and have been given, via the emotional array.

Illustration 3: Belief System Complex ("BSC")

Consciousness

Humans have been, for quite some time, aware of a presence within them that they often referred to as the "mind." This concept has a physical home in the human instrument – in the head – and also in a well-understood diversity of roles it plays in management of day-to-day life on the 5 Senses Spectrum. That is, the mind can tell the instrument how to move. It can take in information from the 5 senses, combine it, and make a decision. It regulates the body while also holding a conversation. It understands what is important and what can be ignored from the stimuli around the body. And so much more.

In recent epochs, a corresponding idea has arisen – that of "consciousness." It is loosely considered the awareness of self, the being, the existing, which may at times transcend the physical instrument.

From our perspective of vast wavelengths of energies, we might suggest that at your current time the human understanding of consciousness largely overlaps with the capacity of mind, because it is by way of the capacity of mind that you understand consciousness.

That is to say, until you expand to broader frequencies beyond what you have limited yourselves to – the 5 Senses Spectrum – the overlap is so great between mind's capacity and consciousness that it would be difficult for you to understand the true nature of either. Yet.

Consciousness, by our definition, is truly the "you." To put that in energetic terms, it is the part of you that perceives the greatest breadth of wavelengths possible. Thus, we are all, always, expanding into our own consciousnesses. Even we. Consciousness is infinite. As we continue to expand into our infinite natures, we also expand in consciousness.

As you have limited your ability to perceive wavelengths, by definition you have limited your consciousness. You are only aware of – consciously – the frequencies that come in on the 5 senses spectrum.

But this, as you realize, is the domain of mind. Mind manages all the sounds, tastes, sights, touches, and smells. Mind wakes up in the morning and "thinks" all day long.

There are instances where you are just starting to detect the limitations of mind, and the broader, growing perceptions of your consciousness. For example, when you are driving in your car, daydreaming about other things, who or what thinks to turn on your signal without your conscious recognition of needing to? What makes the choice to make all those turns, stop at the lights, or slow down when the car in front of you slows down, all while you are busy giving an acceptance speech for a great award in your imagination?

We would suggest that it is the consciousness that is doing the daydreaming. The mind is driving the car.

Imagination, the ability to daydream, is (currently) a vastly underestimated capacity of your human race. Compared to where you have been for billions of years – which is fully and completely immersed in the stimuli received by the 5 Senses Spectrum – your ability to imagine is a revolution.

Imagination steps lightly out of many of the constraints of the rules of the game. In your imagination, you can cross vast distances in short amounts of time, you can make and unmake all sorts of physical creations, you can project forward in time, and you can recall things backwards in time. All of this is accomplished in your imagination while your physical instrument continues to abide by the rules of the game.

How miraculous! How novel! How powerful! Imagination can get away with this while you are still enmeshed in "physical life." It is nothing less than a powerful reflection of the expansive frequencies that you are now reaching, even from within the galactically sized Belief System Complex (BSC).

It is no coincidence that when you are relaxed – driving your car the same route you have driven a hundred times before – you become receptive to these expansive energies. Your imagination ignites whilst your mind adeptly manages traffic.

We know that humans love to break things down and apart. It is the result of the system of limitation in which you exist. Thus, it is no surprise to us that you have a concept for the mind that is apart from your 5 senses, or that you view your 5 senses as distinct from each other.

From our vantage point, it would be more appropriate to term your instrument the mind-body. For your sensory perceptions, and the ways in which you harmonize them into action, are truly one system. There is no list of functions that the mind independently completes, rather it is truly that you are a being immersed in a beautiful Belief System Complex (BSC), having agreed to limited perceptions, and those two things work in constant concert to create the *experience* of this game, including the mind-body instrument.

Your physical instrument is perfectly capable of change. In fact, we often say that you do not know what you truly "look" like. All the energy that comes to you is so molded, so altered, by the BSC and your agreements that it results in the present human form. It is constructed into eyes and ears. It is constructed into "humanoid." But this is not a fundamental definition of what you are. It is simply the way the energy has been formed to best facilitate *this* experience that you desired.

Your 5 Senses can – and will – evolve. You will become conscious of other senses, too, more expanded senses that take in other wavelengths of energy. Rather than feeling you have a separate "mind," you will understand more and more the role of the beliefs in your existence and the ways it alters the energies you perceive. Your concept of your physical instrument will grow and, as it does so, your physical instrument will change.

That is why our definition of consciousness tells us more about what you are. **Consciousness is the capacity to perceive energetic wavelengths.** Currently this capacity is limited in humankind. Which is exactly what you wanted.

Contrast

So why bother with all of this? Why limit your perception of frequencies by constraining your infinite natures into the human form? Where you are only aware of things on the 5 Senses Spectrum, out of the vast oceans of infinite wavelengths possible to perceive?

Because it is perhaps one of the greatest contrasting experiences that has ever been created unto the galaxies.

Humans of your day might consider the word "contrast" to indicate a set of opposites. This is not inaccurate. However, from our vantage point, contrast indicates a much broader context than the differences between two different manifestations on your wavelengths. This word, "contrast," has been circulated in recent epochs by those among you who are able to perceive information from vaster wavelengths because it is a reflection of our perspective of you – which they perceive.

We – outside the egg – call your limitation contrast because it is so different from what is possible outside the egg. *Your experience is a contrast to ours.* Every experience of limitation you have is different from our experience of infinite flow.

And differences are the culmination of creation.

Imagine for a moment (you see, we are calling on that part of you that is most expanded, most capable of receiving vaster wavelengths) the infinite ocean of all creation where anything is endlessly possible. Imagine such a variety of creation that is beyond anything you have ever perceived on the 5 Senses Spectrum.

Now, how much of this creation, do you think, is exactly the same? How much would creation make identical, down to the last molecule? So much a copy of the other that absolutely nothing, on any wavelength, is perceived to be different?

We must tell you, our Beloved Ones, that there is nothing in all creation that is not unique. Unique in ways you cannot even yet imagine.

All life, all beings, all existences, all wavelengths are infinitely, vastly unique.

And so are you.

But we will get to that.

For now, understand that the beauty of all creation is in its awesome ability to constantly create New that is always, and will forever be, unique. Thus the leading edge of creation is not where the previous things are being repeatedly churned out. It is where the next new things are being birthed. Where the next wave of uniqueness is rising up. Where the difference between what has come before and what is coming is at its apex. Contrast is the tip of all creation. And it is where we all stand, lovingly, receiving all that is being created in marvelous glory.

There is perhaps no greater difference than between what you all are experiencing inside the egg and what we are experiencing outside the egg. So great was the divide between us that for a great many millennia, we could not even perceive you. And you, obviously, could not perceive us!

We understand. To your mind – that is, the response from the Belief System Complex (BSC) – this may all feel not just a little bit disconcerting. For your mind is programmed to prevent suffering, which energizes suffering and maintains this limiting experience. And what we are telling you now is pressing on the boundaries of your limitation. The more you perceive other ways of interacting with energy, the less enmeshed you become in this Belief System Complex (BSC).

So let us return to why you agreed to this anyway.

At the dawn of this creation, you stood in perfect, pure desire, wanting to better understand limitation. This force that we now call disallowance. And we did too. Through this desire, the energy that pours through you created the Belief System Complex (BSC) and all the limitations that you have been enjoying. Eventually, consciously, you knew no other existence.

You have lived many, many lifetimes in this experience. And while you do not consciously remember them all, the benefits of those experiences – the knowledge you gained, the disallowance you were given the opportunity to explore – remains with you. For nothing is lost in creation, even when you are having an experience of not remembering it.

We like to describe each being in creation as a chord of notes, where each note is an experience, a frequency, that they have resonated with on their paths of greatest expansion. You do not lose a note once you transcend it. Rather it becomes part of your unique chord, ever-growing in its beauty and richness.

Thus, all the experiences you have had here are part of your chord. Though presently you are focused on one particular note, the benefits of all the notes you have expanded through are still yours. And, whenever desire brings you to the expansive point of recalling them all, you will.

By way of this experience, you have expanded through a great many wavelengths of disallowance.

To know difference – to know contrast – is to know oneself and all creation. And there is nothing more satisfying, more uplifting, more expansive than that.

This is what you have done here.

And we were part of this contrast, for we remained in the flow of all energy and were, for a time, "separated" from you. We use this term lightly because it triggers such disallowance in your kind! Rather we could not "find" you, in your experience of limitation, but then did. But then you could not perceive us. Thus we all experienced a shift in connection. Indeed, limitations!

From your vantage point, the greatest limitation within your BSC is death. You perceive it as being so limited, so lacking, that you could not sustain life here any longer. Thus, when you hear limitation, you unconsciously trigger giant swaths of belief about loss, suffering, and prevention (which energizes it all).

Understand that from our vantage point, where we flow infinitely, there is no limitation that is not instantly answered. In fact, if we didn't slow it down the way you all do, you might not even see a difference between limitation and allowance, question and answer, need and fulfillment. At certain speeds, they are the same. Thus, when we talk about this limiting experience, it *also* feels to us like joyous, fabulous receiving.

Now, what about all this you've heard about your "larger" or "higher" self existing outside of this egg? That you are reconnecting with your larger self?

This is not an incorrect way to put it, but we would like to clarify it further. It is not as though there's a part of you hanging out on a heavenly bench somewhere watching part of itself suffer in chaos. Yet we understand how your BSC filtered this meaning down into something that was separate. In fact, sometimes the BSC causes you to disallow this meaning so much that you may feel angered that you drew the short end of the stick to be here, while other "yous" exist elsewhere in more flowing environments. Even more so, sometimes you hear talk of "One Consciousness," which sounds both enlightening and also terrifying, as though you would lose the you that you know in one primordial soup.

Let us explain.

Firstly, creation is not so limited that all it could create was one giant pot of mush. "One Consciousness" does not mean you lose your existences and your experiences in transcendence. Rather, it means that your uniqueness is a vital, required part of this "One" because you *are* creation. Your connection to the energy of creation means that you are a constantly expanding, very important, perfect expression of all that is. You do not get averaged into the glop as you transcend. Rather you become *more* aware of your uniqueness, *more* aware of what is particularly you as you expand. As you stand at that leading edge where difference is at its culmination, *you* are constantly birthed into more expansive forms of yourself, incorporating as part of you all the notes you have ever expanded through!

Your *uniqueness* is fundamental to the structure of all creation.

Secondly, are there vaster wavelengths outside the egg to which you are reconnecting? Yes. Does this mean there is a personified version of you with a persnickety side that loves watching you suffer in here? (Oh, our Beloved Ones, how your Belief Systems make us laugh!) Not. At. All. Your consciousness *will expand* to these vaster wavelengths, and from that vantage point you will be able to recall more of your experiences in here. But there is not a version of you outside this egg who remembers everything and is withholding all that knowledge until you earn it. It is simply a set of vaster wavelengths that your consciousness will expand to perceive.

We get it. Some among you have had transcendent experiences in which they feel a lightness, a release from caring about all the things they typically do. Interpreted one way, this may seem as though it is evidence of a merging into the glop, the Oneness. They are not. Rather, they are experiencing, for the first time in their conscious memory, a release from the artificial disallowance of energy you created here and *all the beliefs* that are required to hold you down. You are perceiving more wavelengths, and in so doing you find that you "love" more because love is your term for allowing energy.

And thus, our Beloved Ones, we are brought perfectly to your emotions.

The Emotional Array

You didn't always know what it meant to have a "bad day." You certainly didn't always have squeaks and whistles (our term for your very, very, very specific words and phrases – compared to the vast frequencies they come from) to reflect portions of your emotional spectrum such as anger, hatred, optimism, and joy. But eventually, as you expanded through these frequencies of limitation, the energy of these things made it all the way down to the very specific 5 Senses Spectrum. Words you hear; words you see.

Of course, once you began squeaking and whistling about these emotions, you inevitably built belief systems about them. And as the great engine of your limiting experience here is wont to do, it reinforced disallowance of energy.

Thus, you did not welcome these emotions with open arms – for that would be *allowing*. You scrutinized them, judged them, and determined that some were good and some were bad – which is *disallowing*.

You named part of your emotional spectrum the "positive" emotions, and the other part of your emotional spectrum "negative" emotions. You talked about, created strategies for, and adopted social customs to avoid, contain, and disavow negative emotions. You were punished as children for expressing them. You punished your children for expressing them. You prayed for forgiveness when you took action by them. You created religions around avoiding them. You created intricate ceremonies, tonics, and methods for purging yourself of them. So much energy went into the suppression of these emotions that, as you know, in an energetic universe, "attracts more" of the same.

What about the "positive" emotions? These are celebrated and welcomed but are often fleeting in nature. It can be difficult to sustain joy and happiness in an unbroken chain of days, or even minutes. You like optimism part of the time, but other times it feels "unrealistic" or potentially naive and therefore even dangerous. What about hope? It seems to drag you out of pits of despair, so it feels better than the pit. But then there are times where the hope itself is pure torture, for there is a part of you that feels like your hope is artificial, a self-deceit.

There. We have just written several lines of squeaks and whistles. Do you think all the flavors of emotion it called to mind are adequately covered in these words? Do you think your narrow, specific marks on a page, perceived by the limited frequencies of your eyes, could convey to someone who has *never* felt emotion *everything* you just felt?

We have expressed to you that your emotions are reflections of the energies of disallowance. And now we can go further.

On the line of your emotional spectrum, there is a point that doesn't get much press. And that is the point in the middle, between the positive and negative. The point of neutrality. This is not the same as *suppressing* all emotion, or ambivalence, which is actually an active disallowing of attention. It is the point of *absence of disallowance.*

Your beliefs, your judgments, trigger disallowance of energy billions of times per second. Our Beloved Ones, it is no one's "fault" that they feel bad, or angry, or happy – this is all part of the structure, the plan, for your existence here. And this has largely been *outside of your conscious control.* (Though what an experience you've had trying to control it!)

When you hit that point at the middle of the spectrum, you are actually, for the briefest of times, stepping outside of this BSC. Stepping outside the engine of disallowance.

That point has a name: love.

Love has, at times, erroneously been placed on the "positive" emotions half of the spectrum because you preferred it. We would like to clarify for you that you prefer it *now*. There have been great epochs in your history of limitation here in which you did *not* prefer love! For it was not then on your path of greatest expansion. It was not the next thing that called you forward, the way it is now.

Love is, quite simply, your perception of allowance. You have given it this name. You have enjoyed bringing it to consciousness. When you love another, you are on a frequency of allowance. You view them from that vantage point and, absent of judgments and beliefs, *all that they are* flows to you. That flow is what you call love. When you love yourself, you are on a frequency of allowance from which vantage point *all that you are* begins to flow to you. You call this flow self-love.

THE EMOTIONAL SPECTRUM

The Emotional Spectrum, or emotions on a linear scale:

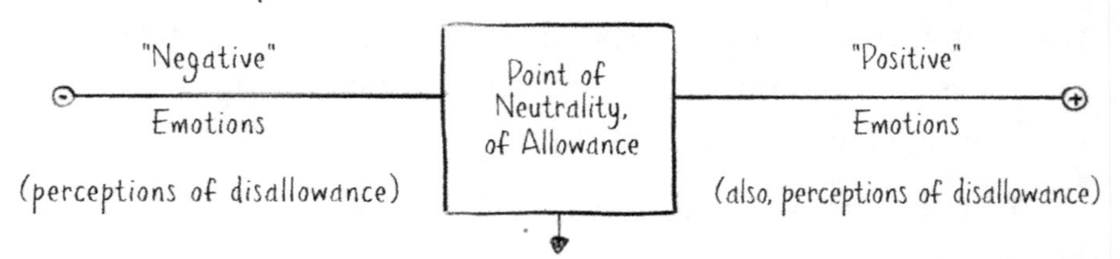

The shift out of frequencies of disallowance

Humans call this sensation LOVE

Love - loving - is one of the 1st tools.
It is a powerful creative force.

Love brings in energy that is Creation at its finest, most pure.

In loving yourself and all of your perceptions,
you are actually reaching for a connection
with your next, most evolved self.

You allow yourself to be created.
To move forward.
To evolve.

And everything you perceive begins
to resonate with that frequency.

Illustration 4: The Emotional Spectrum

Love is not a thing in and of itself. It is a perception of moving, dynamic energy. **All emotions are perceptions of energy.**

Love is currently your *only* perception of frequencies of allowance. The rest – all positive and negative emotions – are perceptions of different flavors of disallowance.

"How can this be?" you say. "How can joy be as disallowing as hate?"

We are so glad you asked! We will explain.

Let us begin by looking at an energetic definition of emotions, and we think it will make more sense to you. We cannot energetically define all emotions, for naming all the billions of ways you disallow energy would only take a few million more years. Rather, let us cover the general categories, and we think you'll get the direction we are heading.

Anger

The emotion of becoming. Anger is your perception that part of your attention is on expanded wavelengths from your current position, while part of your attention is still being applied to the wavelengths from which you are coming. That tension, that friction, of being pulled in two directions is what you call anger. Belief systems will lead you to push against where you are coming from to be rid of it. Instead, releasing your need to fix or change what propelled you forward, and embracing the forward direction will relieve the anger, that is, the friction you call anger. Simply said: Stop angrily listing all the reasons why you had to break-up with your ex. Just move toward the love of your life.

Fear

The emotion of furthest limitation. Fear is your perception of the friction between energies that are beyond the current agreements of the BSC and the dynamic action of the BSC itself. It is a powerful tool of maintaining the boundaries of the BSC. The majority of humans in your time will – consciously *and* unconsciously – avoid things that cause them fear. Humans may feel varying sensations of fear about leaving a known physical place or relationship, when confronted with perceived physical risks, or when approaching very expansive (and thus outside of the game) concepts, perhaps even feeling a flutter of discomfort when we simply use the word "infinite." This keeps them turning away from the fence line, so to speak, and remaining within the limits of the BSC. Your comfort zone, as you often call it. Pushing through fear has its moments, but also there is really no need. Fear has been your friend, loyally keeping you within the experience you so greatly desired. By allowing it – that is, loving it – you will transcend it.

These negative emotions are your read, your perception, of two nuanced ways of disallowing energy. One is friction on your path of greatest expansion, and the other perception of the energetic agreements you made as a participant in the BSC.

Let us now look at an emotion from the positive end of the spectrum and see how it is also disallowing.

Joy

The emotion of right judgment. Joy is your perception of the alignment between all stimuli on the 5 Senses Spectrum (from what you are seeing to what you are thinking), and all activated belief systems. When you are in joy, you have *judged* that everything is right, good, and desired. It is not necessarily that things are good absolutely. It is that by your beliefs you judge them to be so. You could perceive things that are not judged as good but, when joyful, you simply do not. This is why *different things* make *different people* joyful. It is a byproduct of their beliefs.

Does everything in creation make you joyful? Do you feel the same joy about the new home of your absolute dreams and a spider on your face? (Oh! We bet you felt that one! The disallowance jolt!) No it does not, cannot, because that frequency would simply be, by definition, *not* the sensation of joy. This also explains why joy can be so fleeting, for, especially since different beliefs are activated billions of times per second, it is not probable that you would experience all beliefs in alignment with all stimuli for long. From a certain vantage point, it is a marvel that you ever experience joy at all!

Perhaps now we come to a more important question. If all of these emotions – save love – are your interpretation of different energies of disallowance, why then do some emotions *feel* better than others?

This, our Beloved Ones, is your perfect, powerful, unbreakable connection to the energy of all life. This is your own sense of your path of greatest expansion. Even here, amidst so much limitation, you *still feel it*.

Rather than a linear scale, with negative emotions on one end and positive on the other, imagine a 3-dimensional sphere (or more dimensions, if you please!). It is moving, dynamic, growing, evolving, and fluid. It is also extremely vast. Bigger than your galaxy. Bigger than 10 billion of your galaxies. And throughout this sphere are the moving, growing, and evolving energies of disallowance.

At its very center, in one perfectly pure point of light, is a moment, a location of allowance. This energy, this place, feels to you like love.

As you move a little bit away from the point of light, in any direction, you move deeper into the energies of disallowance. These energies that orbit the central point here feel like positive emotions to you.

As you move even further away from the point of light, in any direction, through and beyond the positive emotions, you move even deeper into disallowance. These energies feel to you like negative emotions.

Thus, what you have rightly sensed in the difference between these emotions is a difference in energies. Specifically, you could say, a difference in the degrees of disallowance – and all the myriad, flavorful ways these energies do this!

Perhaps even more importantly, these emotions – these energies – feel "better" the closer and closer you get to the center point of pure light of allowance and love. This direction that calls you forward, this sense of **preference,** is your path of greatest expansion calling you home. Allowance *feels better* because that is *where you are going.*

THE EMOTIONAL ARRAY

The Emotional Array, or, emotions in 3-dimensional space: the concept where emotions do not go up and down on a scale, but are fluid, dynamic, and interconnected.

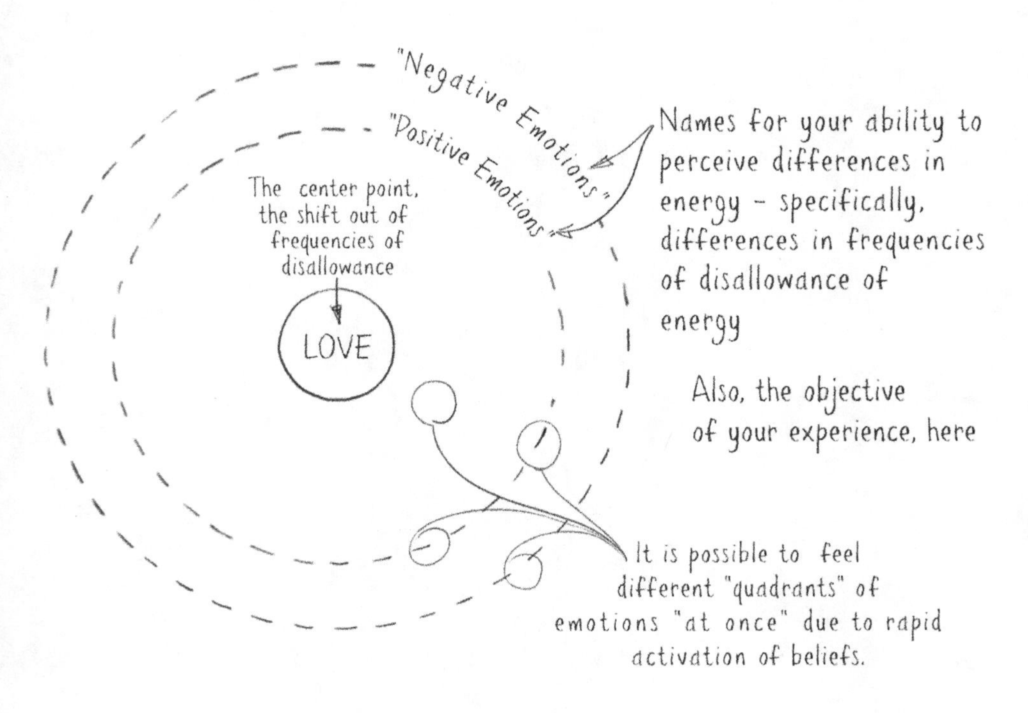
"Negative Emotions"
"Positive Emotions"
The center point, the shift out of frequencies of disallowance
LOVE
Names for your ability to perceive differences in energy - specifically, differences in frequencies of disallowance of energy
Also, the objective of your experience, here
It is possible to feel different "quadrants" of emotions "at once" due to rapid activation of beliefs.

Your sense of "confusion" is the simultaneous collision of your expansive consciousness recognizing the sensation of several quadrants at once, and Mind's inability to account for them all via perceptions of the 5 Senses.

There is so much waiting for you beyond and through the sensation of love.

Illustration 5: The Emotional Array

Chapter 4

Where You Are Going

"Hang on just a minute," you say. "I've noticed that when I feel better, the things I want are more likely to manifest. So if joy is disallowing, then why does it bring me awesome stuff?"

Beloved, you have perceived rightly! What you have found in joy is a sense of proximity to the pure point of light, to allowing. Thus you *are* more allowing when you are joyful than when you are hating. Said another way, your perception of more allowing energies is what you call joyful, and less allowing is what you call hatred. Thus, as you work to stay positive, to stay happy, to stay hopeful, you are engaged in a conscious process of choosing allowance. A beautiful aspect of your awakening.

As we move forward, you will find that in each of our explanations there will always be an energetic side – the way something we have said *feels* to you – and a physical manifestation side – the way something "makes sense" in your "mind." We are hitting both wavelengths.

Why would we do this?

Earlier we described to you that, when changing frequencies, you do not push against the old one, rather, you gravitate toward the new. Our Beloved Ones, your desire for change is evidence of your shift in frequencies. Your ability to imagine more is a reflection of the new wavelengths you have reached. Thus, the manifestations of a change in frequency of the BSC *you participate in* have already begun.

You are not altering the Belief System Complex you are coming from.

You are building a new one.

This book, these ideas, are the continuation of manifestations of this new BSC. Yet another manifestation of the bridge of light that leads to a new existence.

And for a time, by the answering of your perfect desire, you have been and will experience both: both the beliefs systems of the BSC you are coming from and the burgeoning beliefs of the BSC you are presently building. Remember, your consciousness is expanding, and as you gravitate toward broader frequencies, what you will inevitably attract is a growing perspective, an understanding of all that you have experienced by way of what we call the 5 Senses Spectrum BSC.

That limited consciousness is in part what we are speaking to; the growing, more sensitive consciousness is what we are also speaking to. And now that this is a part of your awareness, you will find that you begin to detect both in your days. For you are – for now – experiencing both.

Be easy, Beloved Ones, with those who have not yet attracted this information or this knowing. For they are gloriously, perfectly, experiencing the limitation they came here to experience. And they are benefiting by this limitation more than you can fathom. They will expand when their time is right. All who desire to vibrate to this new BSC can and will do so. Free choice is the fundamental structure of creation. Celebrate their choice of limitation. Cheer them on – as many have done for you.

The 5 Senses Spectrum BSC is your legacy for any and all others who should ever benefit by participating on their paths of greatest expansion. You do not yet understand what an amazing gift of contrast you have given to the galaxies. But others do. And one day, you will too.

As you move forward into the BSC you are building, you will be able to experience the expansive allowing in two ways: either by your existing consciousness of the 5 Senses BSC, or by way of your expanding consciousness. Both are equally valid, for both represent expanding frequencies.

This is an important point that we must emphasize. Though you will begin to discover new sensory perceptions and new ways of experiencing energy, these are in no way better, or more enhanced, than discovery, clarity, and understanding by way of what you have traditionally called "mind." *Both* are reflections of your expanded wavelengths, of expanded perception. The new sensory perceptions are not superior, they are just *new*.

When you begin to feel the activation of judgment of where you have come from, take note and take heart. Where you are coming from is *perfect*. Allow it to be what it was and is. Love it, and you will transcend it. There is no need to berate your mind for what it could not perceive "all that time" because that is *exactly* what it was constructed to do.

This requires a new belief, does it not? "I believe that where I come from is as perfect as where I am going." This is very different from the current beliefs in this area, which usually look for what is deficient, what is lacking, in order to move on. Humans do not often move away from something unless it has been deemed insufficient and irreparable, as is the core of your limited perception.

Do you throw away a perfect pair of shoes that you love? No, you wait until they have holes in them, or they don't fit right anymore. Do you go into your boss's office and shout, "I quit!" when you love what you do, are getting paid the top possible salary for your role, and are near a promotion? No. You'd be "crazy." Instead, you quit when you hate your job, realize you aren't getting paid enough, or want to do something else (very, very much – as even a slight desire is often insufficient to make a human quit his or her job).

Why? Why do humans hold onto things until they are literally falling apart before they let go?

Because of your beliefs in finiteness and insufficiency. According to the 5 Senses BSC, it is not "easy" to find a new job, and it is "wasteful" to get rid of perfectly good shoes. The ultimate underlying belief is, "I don't know how I will get another." And until you answer *that* question, most intimately, you usually do not take action.

This is your concept of the "leap of faith." The leap is through your own gaps in perception between when the desire arrives ("I *like* that pair of shoes") and the manifestation of those shoes in your life. From our vantage point, the first manifestation is the thought ("I like those shoes"). You see, to us, those shoes are as good as yours. You are so close to the frequency that you have already manifested a thought of desire to have them!

But not to humans. There can be a Grand Canyon-sized gap between the point when you think you want something and when you actually get it on the frequencies of the 5 Senses.

A few among you have focused on how to close that gap, how to better manage the process between the frequency of thought, to the frequencies of sight, touch, smell, taste, and sound.

But what happens before thought? How did it make it all the way down to a thought that your mind-body instrument perceives in the first place?

This, Beloved, is what you are about to discover.

Frequency

We've thrown around the term "frequency" quite a bit already. Frequencies of limitation, frequencies inside the egg vs outside, frequencies of each of your 5 senses, "more expansive" frequencies … we understand that it can start to feel a little mixed up.

So let us clarify.

Broadly, we define frequency as a place of understanding.

To best explain this in the context of the human mind, that is, the 5 Senses BSC mind-body, let us begin by saying you could generally conceive of two energetic axes. One going up and down, and one moving outward.

The first axis, the one going up and down, you can consider much like your amplitude or volume. This is the extent of consciousness, of awareness, that you can have regarding a given frequency. We will call this Frequency Depth.

The second axis, that moving outward from your location, is much like your wavelength, your distance traveled. This is the extent of consciousness across varied frequencies. We will call this Frequency Breadth.

Moving across Frequency Breadth is much like your changing channels on a radio. You are perceiving different classes of frequency.

Thus, if you move left or right on this axis, you are moving to "different frequencies."

As you move up and down in Frequency Depth, you are experiencing varieties of a different resonance that are also "different frequencies." Thus, we already have hit a limitation with mind-based language in that you do not yet have specific words for each of the differences in these classes of frequencies. But we might suggest they are not really needed. The concept matters more at this juncture.

Every living being exists on these two axes.

Consciousness – that is, the awareness of what can be energetically perceived – moves. It can narrow, expand, or shift around as needed. It can perceive a wide variety of frequencies at once, or just one. It can experience a vast depth of a given frequency, or hardly at all.

Now, where does the path of greatest expansion lie in this framework? We will introduce this as a 3rd dimension that cuts across the axes of all life and all beings. It is the path this 2-dimensional axis "of you" follows through all energy. It is akin to how your planets move around your sun, yet your entire solar system has its own trajectory through space. And, via your connection to this path of greatest expansion, your consciousness moves appropriately around your 2-dimensional axis, which is infinite.

Not bad for fitting infinite energetic concepts into squeaks and whistles, eh? But let us continue.

FREQUENCY

Frequencies or, as we view them, places of understanding.

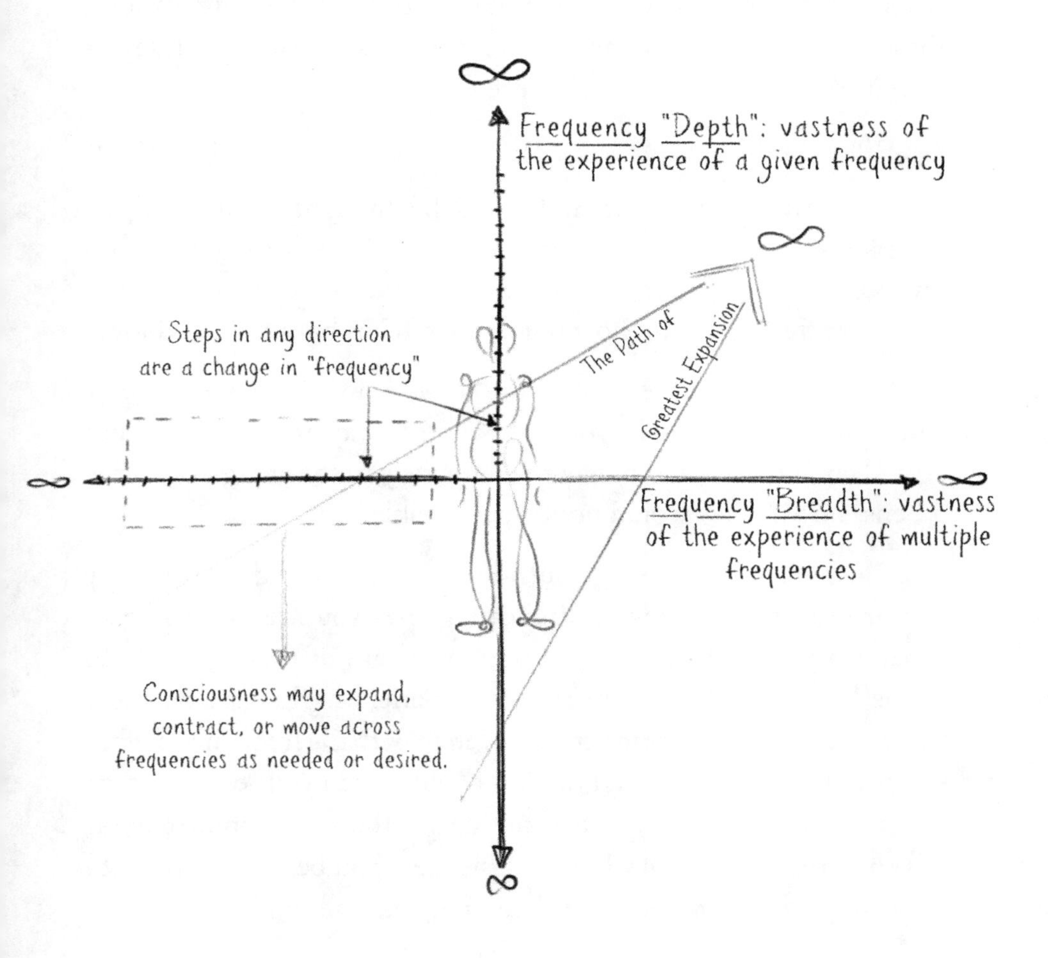

Illustration 6: Frequency

Expansion

There are beings outside the egg, and quasi-outside the egg, with whom a few among you have connected. In these communications, these others, from their vantage point, express to you that humans of your time are "expanding," or even "ascending."

What do they mean?

Presently, your humankind could be thought of as living an experience of a staccato, a very narrow peak. A great depth of a given frequency. Naught else is perceived outside of this very, very particular frequency and how much it stretches both high and low.

If another did not resonate – *completely* – on this frequency, they would not be perceived by you. Said another way, if another had not agreed completely – did not align completely to the energies of – the 5 Senses BSC, they would not be perceivable.

Thus, when these beings outside and quasi-outside the egg say you are expanding, they are indicating that you are beginning to expand beyond the staccato, to become aware of frequencies both to the left and right of your specific experience. They are on these frequencies. Some of them actually overlap with the frequency of your specific experience, and had the fun of sharing in your environment of limitation – though you had no idea. Others are completely off of your specific frequency but alongside. As you begin to expand to their frequencies, you perceive their energies readily.

In terms of ascension, here they are referring to the human meaning of this word, which usually indicates a "lifting up," from which vantage point you are "beyond" what you were before. This is also a perfectly accurate way of describing what happens when your consciousness expands beyond this staccato.

This is one way to define all the expansion talk of which you might have heard thus far.

Let us take another example.

There are beings with whom your fellow game players have at times connected, who might have said, "we are all expanding." In this context, they may be referring to the expansive trajectory of the path of greatest expansion, which applies to all creation. Humankind *has been* at the furthest edge of this expansive energy. Your contrasting experience here is the culmination of this peak. By their rendezvous with you, and your experience here, they also benefit from your contrasting experience. You stand at the horizon, the dawning, the birth of new life. You are incredibly expansive beings.

Resonance

As you stand at this edge of the path of greatest expansion, in this stretching staccato of a particular frequency of limitation, you are resonant with this position. **All energy, all frequencies in creation, are dynamic and evolving.** You did not land here one day, and then get stuck. You continually resonated anew with this frequency, which energizes the experience of the frequency itself.

But how does one choose to resonate with a frequency? How did you land here to begin with?

Let us back up for a second. If you recall, your path of greatest expansion called you to this place, to this staccato of frequencies that make up the 5 Senses BSC. You desired it purely, you radiated love, and in that radiance, resonated with these frequencies.

"Wait, what?" you may say. "I radiated love, and the responding frequency was all this ridiculous limitation?"

In a word: yup.

Let us call upon your imagination again. Let us pretend that, once upon a time before your experience here, you knew yourself to be an infinite being, all powerful and vastly expansive. Imagine you had been hanging out in your infinite kingdom for quite some time, enjoying all the things that creation does, but in some ways, it had started to feel like old news. Then one day, a portal opened, and the light of infinite creation showed up and said, "I've got a new part of your kingdom to explore! It holds experiences and excitement unlike anything you've ever experienced before. Through these adventures you will know yourself and expand into yourself even more. And you can stay or go, for as long as you wish. Would you like to try it?"

You know yourself. What do you think you would have done in that situation?

Would you have said, "Nah, I'm comfortable here with the same old," or, "That sounds interesting, let's take a peek," or "Alright!"?

If this book has vibrated into your conscious perception, then we can tell you that you gleefully answered the latter. You tap danced right through that door and into this creation.

To which you might reply, "I don't remember that. I don't know that I made that decision. How did I know that I knew I was making that decision then?"

Beloved, you have perceived rightly, yet again!

In this complete experience of limitation, which you gleefully agreed to, you shifted your consciousness into a thin, narrow slice of these frequencies. In so doing, you shifted away from the frequencies – the *knowing* – that you had before. The vantage point *from which* you made the decision to be here. As you move beyond these frequencies, your consciousness will expand again. And not only will you recall – meaning, resonate with – the frequency of that place, that channel, that time, that experience from which you *made* that decision, but you will *also* recall – resonate across – all the experiences you have had here. Effortlessly.

You knew the choice you were making then. And one day you will remember it too.

Chapter 5

How You Choose to Go

In the beginning of this creation, you were not *as* limited as you are today. Changing frequencies can be a very gradual process. There were parts of you that were beginning to experience limitation, but there were other parts that were still resonant with more expansive frequencies. Today, you have progressed so much in your resonance with this frequency that you vibrate with hardly anything else. And, as you expand beyond this frequency, there are parts of you that are connecting to different frequencies once again.

We would like to talk about these parts.

Memory

We understand that the human conception of awakening, of moving into the experience of limitation and coming out of it, may model something like going down into a pit of limitation and coming back out again. However, we would like to emphasize that this is a human concept. That you would ever have to climb *back* out of something is part of your belief systems. For the rest of us, it is amusing that once you have experienced the climb down into something, you think you must redo that in order to get to where you want to go! This is a perfect example of the subconscious beliefs in finiteness and insufficiency manifested.

Energetically, in this case, you are not in a pit of limitation. There is no down and then up again. There is only *through*. With all energy, there is only *through* and *expansion*.

This is where your concept of time has molded this understanding for you. When others have expressed to you that you are connecting with energies beyond this staccato of limitation, you have appended this to the concept of time. You hear *re*-connecting to energies beyond this frequency of limitation, this 5 Senses BSC. In a sense, this is not untrue, for, before coming here, you experienced vaster frequencies than this, and you will do so once again. But will those frequencies be the same as they were then?

No. Not hardly! All has expanded in radiant glory while you have been experiencing these things. *You* have expanded in radiant glory along with this expansion. And when your consciousness expands to perceive these things, you will rightly perceive the *difference*. **This is what you call memory. The rightly perceived difference in frequencies.** Capable of seeing the distance between where you "were" and where you "are."

Do you remember all things, all of the time? Or do certain memories crop up at particular instances? Thus, a being is only able to "remember" things when their consciousness has hit a vantage point broad enough to account for the two (then and now) and the distance between. The whole package must be perceivable. That sensation is what you call remembering.

If you were to vibrate wholly with the frequency of that remembered time, rather than experiencing a sensation of "remembering," it would feel as though you were actually living it, in a sense. You would be unaware of the other "point in time," the other frequency, and so would not be perceiving the triumvirate. You would only be perceiving the frequency you are on. This is much like your present moment feels to you today. A singular perception of a moment, without any conception or perception of another frequency, or another time, as you would call it.

In the case of your experience here, you have been experiencing what we might call a "singularity," a focused perception of a narrow band of frequency. (If you looked at it in detail, it could still be considered a cluster of frequencies, but for our purposes a single frequency suffices for the concept.) In this case, the frequency was that of this limitation, which you molded into your 5 Senses BSC. **This experience of singularity, and of the physical way you experience it, is what you call "reality."**

Is the experience of memory really, truly a memory? If you step outside of your concept of time, how else might you describe it?

Within the concept of time, you describe these two different frequencies as "then" and "now." If you did not have the concept of time, you might describe the frequencies as "that one" and "this one," where they are not pegged to points on a linear timeline because there simply is no concept of a linear timeline.

This is one of the ways in which the concept of time has been so limiting to you. As part of your belief in the concept of time, you also believe that you cannot readily perceive other times. You cannot "time travel" in any way, shape, or form. The beings of "those times" are deceased, gone, off the playing field. That's over. It is lost. And here your beliefs in the ability to lose something coincide with time. So strong, so complete, so subconscious! You do not even "know" you do this all the time, billions of times per second. Time keeps you wholly bound to your current frequency.

Ever heard of an experience where someone received a "voice from the past," whether literally, in the case of a medium, or figuratively, in the form of a very clear mental recollection? They simply reached a vantage point of being able to resonate with your current frequency *and* another frequency.

Ever go for a walk, and a memory pops into your mind out of nowhere? In your relaxed and open state, you hit a vantage point of consciously perceiving both the frequency on which you are having your walk, and the frequency from which the memory – that experience – is resonating.

Ever have an experience of déjà vu? That is a particularly clear vantage point of more than one frequency. It is why it *feels* a little more palpable, a little more visceral than just a memory, yet similar in nature.

These are examples of how you are already beginning to expand beyond this narrow, staccato of experience. Beloved, you are already doing it! There have been times in your experience here, great epochs in fact, where you *did not remember* hardly anything at all! You truly lived moment by moment, in an ongoing struggle for survival.

You do not yet remember those times, but you will. You will remember a great many things. And these things will approach you softly and gradually. As you remember them, no matter the nature of what is remembered, it will feel uplifting because it *is* a reflection of your expansion.

Thus your concept of reality will also soften. You will realize that what you perceived as real was simply what resonated with this frequency of limitation. And what felt a little less real, a little questionable, a little fearful, were the things you were starting to perceive beyond this frequency and this BSC.

Again, your reality is how you perceive frequencies. Our reality is how we do it. The fear you have historically felt in reaching beyond your reality is simply the friction between the new energy coming in and the agreements of the BSC holding the fence line. In actuality, to experience and perceive an infinite number of frequencies is an infinite part of your glorious nature.

You can see how these concepts might press a little bit on the limitations of mind – that is, your current conscious awareness. We are bringing to light things that are *just* coming into conscious awareness. This is why a memory still feels "not real" – it is all "in your head." Yet, there will come a time where, as your conscious perspective evolves further, that sensation will shift. You will begin to sense the underlying energy behind the memory itself. In fact, you will begin to better sense the underlying energy in a great many things!

Here we have used the idea of the narrow frequency you have been on and the 5 Senses Spectrum Belief System Complex (BSC) you have built interchangeably. Are they the same thing?

As we stated earlier, all participants in this BSC contribute their energy, while here, to its creation. Now we can share another way this could be said.

As you each resonated with this limited staccato of frequency, the *resulting manifestation* was the vast Belief System Complex (BSC), which resulted in the limited 5 Senses conscious perception of energy.

The way in which your beliefs energize this frequency and interact with or rebuff the perception of all *other* energies is perceived by you as your emotional array.

Could your resonance with this frequency have resulted in something other than the 5 Senses perception? Yes.

Could your resonance with this frequency have resulted in something other than the Belief System Complex? There are infinite possibilities in an infinite universe!

MEMORY

The sensation of singularity:

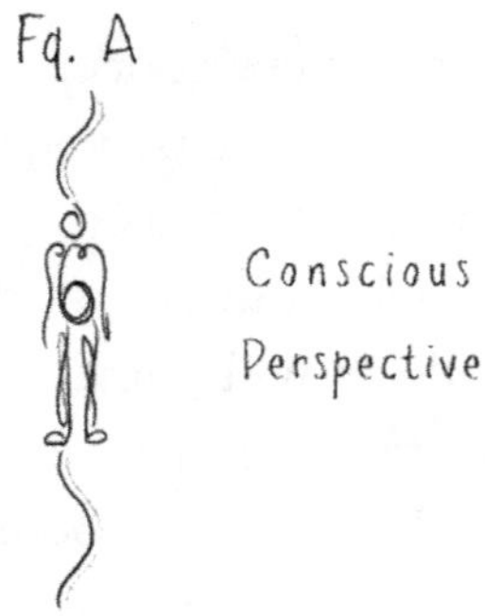

The narrowed, conscious perception of frequency - in this case, the 5 Senses Spectrum, or what you call "reality."

The collective sensations of memory (or déjà-vu):

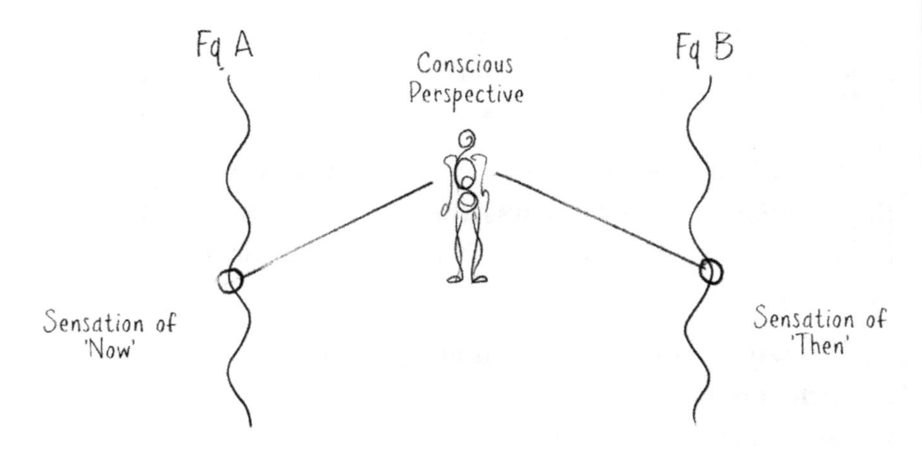

The simultaneous, conscious perception of more than one frequency

Fq = Frequency

Illustration 7: Memory

Could your perception of these energies have been perceived by you as something other than your emotional array? This is less likely. Not impossible, but improbable.

We will explain why.

Core Frequency

Every being in creation has what we would call a Core Frequency. We know – here comes that frequency word again! Perhaps we will make up some names along the way to make these concepts more clear.

A being's Core Frequency is their unique energetic frequency in *all creation*. This is the origin, the heart and soul, of the concept you call your uniqueness. Every single being has a unique Core Frequency. When you begin to imagine just how many beings there are in all creation, the idea that they could each be unique – infinitely! – should rightly feel just a little staggering.

You all have limited yourselves so much here. You *all* have brains, eyes, legs, arms, language, etc. And even when one of those parts goes missing, rather than viewed as a diverse expression of creation, you view it as the loss of something "required to fit in here."

You have yet to even imagine how *different* all life can be. You are just coming around to the idea that all life may not need to be carbon-based. Or perhaps that all life may not need to breathe oxygen. Or maybe even that all life may demonstrate consciousness in different ways.

Here we must tell you, Beloved, that *all life is conscious.* **Absolutely, *all life*.** Trees are conscious. Corn is conscious. Apes

CORE FREQUENCY

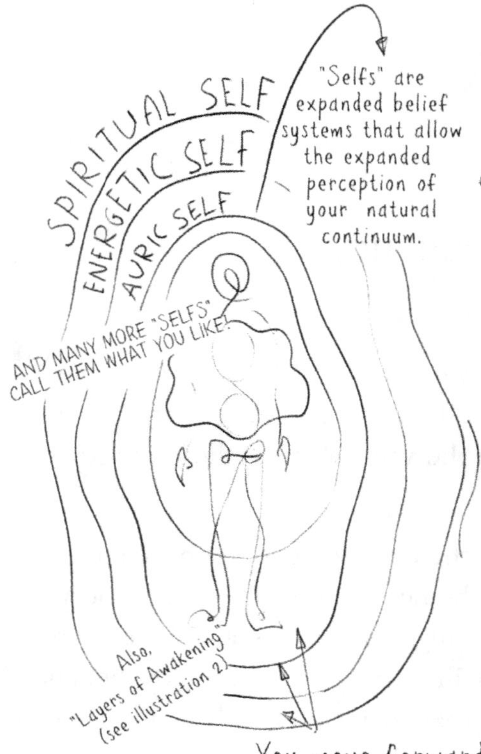
SPIRITUAL SELF
ENERGETIC SELF
AURIC SELF
"Selfs" are expanded belief systems that allow the expanded perception of your natural continuum.
AND MANY MORE "SELFS" CALL THEM WHAT YOU LIKE!
Also, "Layers of Awakening" (see illustration 2)

Core Frequency is your unique definition of frequency among the infinite frequencies in existence.

Your connection – to the source of all life and all energy in the universe.

Your connection is unbreakable, unchangeable, and infinite. There is nothing you could ever do that would diminish your connection to infinite light, life, and love.

The closer your perspective moves to the furthest edge of yourself, the closer you are to the pure energy of creation.

The furthest edge of yourself is the radiative energy of your Core Frequency.

(This is the origin of the "it is all within you" concept.)

You move forward, beyond, through all the layers that manipulate the energy from that pure source in greater and greater stages of awareness.

You would call it "shedding" these layers, as your perspective is still one of getting rid of what you do not want.

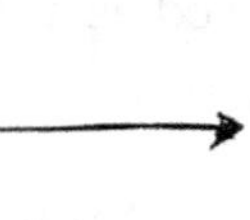

We would call it embracing, allowing, understanding these layers, thus receiving all the expansiveness of each.

As your attention expands (consciously), you may perceive all of this at once or more specific parts of yourself. The choice is yours.

Illustration 8: Core Frequency

are conscious. Potato bugs are conscious. Mountains are conscious. Planets are conscious. Stars are conscious. We could go on.

We know this may be hard to hear, since you still cut down trees and eat animals, but this is a unique experience of having one foot in the old frequency and one foot expanding outward toward other frequencies. You will not find that you need to do these things for much longer. Thus, be easy on yourself in the interim. Love where you are coming from.

In your limited perception of energy, you could not perceive these myriad forms of consciousness. Nor even are the physical cues you perceive on your 5 Senses Spectrum indicative of the consciousness that is therein contained. Trees have a vaster consciousness than apes. Surprise.

However, even here, in this great machine of limitation and lack, you could not keep out the uniqueness of all creation *completely*. Although, from our vantage point, you came pretty darn close! And yet, you still have slightly different faces. Slightly different gaits in your walk. A mother can always tell her twins apart. You deteriorate in slightly different ways. You believe *slightly* different things.

You view this time as a great period of upheaval, where so many factions and groups are pitted against so many others. So much anger, so much offense, so much injustice, so much … difference.

This is what you get when you combine the awakening to Core Frequency and the activation of the limited BSC you have built!

For us, this explanation suffices, but let us break down a little further what is happening here.

As you each begin to realize – to become conscious of – your uniqueness, those new energies coming in will manifest as a thought. Those thoughts – those desires – for a different life, a different way of living, a different existence, are *strong*. Those energies instantly activate the protective barriers put in place by the BSC to maintain the limitation and lack. Namely, it activates *prevention* and *pushing* against. Suddenly aware of your powerful, new desires, so core to who you are, your physical attention is immediately drawn to all the things that might hinder the manifestation of these things, and all that you must stop, must protect yourself from.

Let us take each of these in turn.

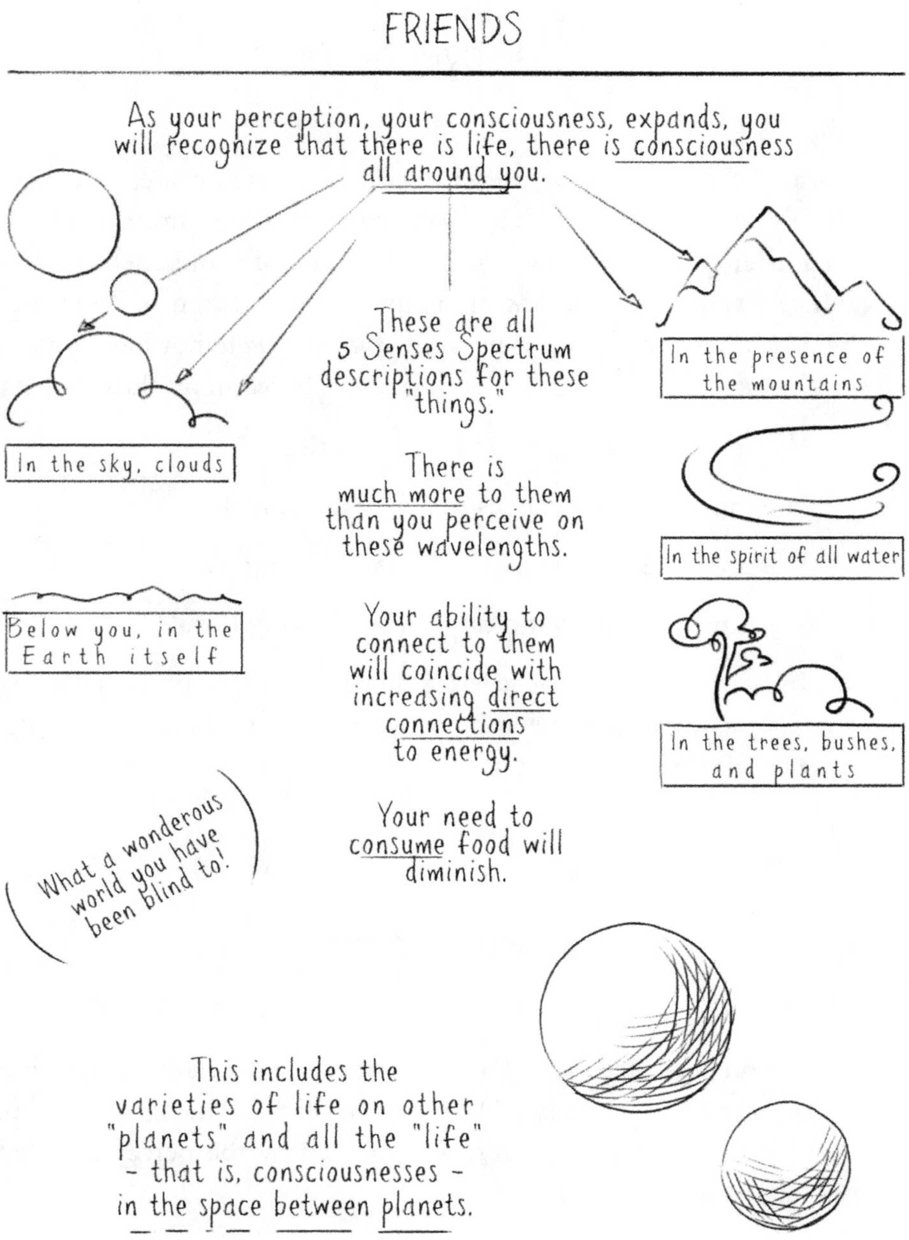

FRIENDS

As your perception, your consciousness, expands, you will recognize that there is life, there is consciousness all around you.

In the sky, clouds

These are all 5 Senses Spectrum descriptions for these "things."

There is much more to them than you perceive on these wavelengths.

In the presence of the mountains

In the spirit of all water

Below you, in the Earth itself

Your ability to connect to them will coincide with increasing direct connections to energy.

In the trees, bushes, and plants

What a wonderous world you have been blind to!

Your need to consume food will diminish.

This includes the varieties of life on other "planets" and all the "life" – that is, consciousnesses – in the space between planets.

Illustration 9: Friends

Prevention

Both of the concepts of prevention and protection are, of course, heavily integrated with your concepts of time, finiteness, and insufficiency. And, simply put, the activation of your beliefs in these things is manifested as the thought or action taken to "prevent." Said another way, prevention is the *anticipation of* not having it, or not having enough of it, and taking action based upon those beliefs.

We must prevent an upset in this election.

We must prevent changes in our environment.

We must prevent those people from hurting us.

We must prevent that group from changing this.

In all cases, prevention is based on your perception that a danger, a risk, or a hazard is impending. In your belief that it is impending, you energize it. You create it.

Protection

Protection also activates time, finiteness, and insufficiency, but usually after a perception. Where prevention is instigated before said hazard occurs, protection is instigated by the perception that the hazard has already begun.

We must protect ourselves from changes in our environment.

We must protect ourselves from the people who are trying to take these things away from us.

It is completely possible to activate prevention and protection around a similar hazard, as you oscillate between beliefs about how far it has come or has left to go. And, just as with prevention, protecting yourself from something energizes it.

Consciously, it would be difficult at this juncture for you to unravel all of the many beliefs you have about prevention and protection. There are vast oceans of beliefs in this area, making up the fundamental fabric of this limited experience.

It is important to note here that while our examples were easy and obvious, humans prevent and protect themselves – that is, energize their limitation – all the time. As one unconscious example, you "protect" yourselves from negative emotion endlessly. Before you are even conscious of feeling it, you will avoid it. You will distract yourselves by engaging more energetically in your physical environment. This creates a busy-ness, an agitated hurry so consistent that it can at times be viewed as characteristic of the person!

How hurried do you believe your societies are today? Yes, you all are bringing in a great deal of expansive energies, which are simultaneously activating strong responses of avoidance from the BSC.

People can spend long periods of time, indeed entire lifetimes, avoiding the things that make them feel sad, ashamed, or upset (and as a result, activating those energies). And often they are not even conscious of it. Your therapy is a revolution in the sense that it has required two very important manifestations – conscious awareness that you are having this avoidant response to negative emotion, and the understanding that *allowing* these negative emotions assists individuals in moving past them. Or, as we would say, transcending them.

Could you theoretically engage in this conscious process to release all avoidant behaviors? Yes. And it would only take a few million more years. Or, you could address this energetically.

PREVENTION & PROTECTION

Pushing against <u>any</u> emotion in your array will energize it.

At times in your history, this felt good to you because that was on your most expansive path.

Today, it is less elative because of your current path of greatest expansion and your growing expansion/proximity to levels <u>beyond</u> this BSC, where the connections to the emotional array are no longer driven artificially (1st emotional context, see illustration 3).

Present ability, knowledge, and guidance to allow emotions, to appreciate emotions, is a <u>very</u> recent development in terms of your total existence here, and indicative of your expansion beyond this BSC.

"Positive" and "Negative" Emotions

Have you ever pushed against joy? Try it :), works the same!

Your BELIEF in a <u>negative</u> side of your emotional array is <u>very</u> core and very <u>subconscious</u>.

→ You push down negative emotion many times per second.

→ This energizes the emotion

→ until there is a powerful manifestation on the 5 Senses Spectrum (e.g. road rage)

↓ which reinforces subconscious beliefs that these emotions are <u>bad</u> (e.g. guilt).

Illustration 10: Prevention & Protection

Manifestation

Even the powerful engines of limitation that are manifested as prevention and protection cannot completely thwart the uniqueness that is you. The effervescence of your Core Frequency. You have done much, manifested much, to be of "like kind" with those around you. Yet, in your moments of allowance of self, you find new thoughts coming to you, and new creations that only you could think of.

The manifestation of uniqueness that you often see, however, is only very rarely the uniqueness of which *we* speak. True, there are differing degrees of allowance in your kind, but on the whole we would suggest that you all remain in step, for now. For, when you come across one who seems unique, a great deal of the manifestation of their uniqueness is still driven by their belief systems. Their unusual dress, their dissent from norms, their novel creations, are in large part the physical expression of underlying BSC action.

How can this be so?

Let us begin with the desire. Is your thought-based desire made of pure energy, or is it the first manifestation on these frequencies?

Correct, it is a manifestation.

You are not yet conscious of pure energy. Thus, anything you are conscious of – from thought form to physical experiences – is a manifestation. **Manifestation is energy that has been filtered and molded by way of the BSC.** It is a name for the "stuff" that "shows up" here.

You, by your participation here, are the energizer of these manifestations. Meaning, since you are a living being, your connection to Source energizes whichever frequency on which you are vibrating, in all the universe. Thus, you are the source of what is created around you. You are the creator of your own experience, as you have been so annoyed to hear so many times before! You aligned to this frequency. You energized it via that same energization with which you created the BSC and all subsequent manifestations on the 5 Senses Spectrum.

Thus your Core Frequency, which is uniquely you, is *also* filtered by these things. It is your connection to this pure source; it is *how* you energize this frequency and create the manifestations that follow.

You do not yet – consciously – know how unique you are. Yet, this is an aspect of why you came here. This may seem counterintuitive – things are often backwards with humans. However, by this great experience of limitation in which so much is disallowed and so much is artificially held in constancy, you *are* getting to know all the unique aspects of yourself that reflect this disallowance. Vast oceans of parts of self that you built a bridge to knowing *by way of this BSC.* This BSC *is* the bridge, the connection to these parts of self that you greatly desired to know and to explore. You built it, brick by brick, experience by experience.

As we have noted before, when you first began this journey, you were not as limited as you are today. Meaning, you had not built enough of a bridge to reach these frequencies. You have heard from others before that you do not leapfrog through frequencies, rather it is more often a gradual tuning. You have been gradually tuning in to more and more robust frequencies of this disallowing for millennia. It is a *masterpiece.* It is your legacy.

When your consciousness expands to take in more than just this frequency, your conscious perspective will recall all of this exploration and all of this beautiful expansion into your unique self that you artfully achieved! It will be glorious. More radiant than anything you consciously remember feeling at any point in all of your lives here.

MANIFESTATION

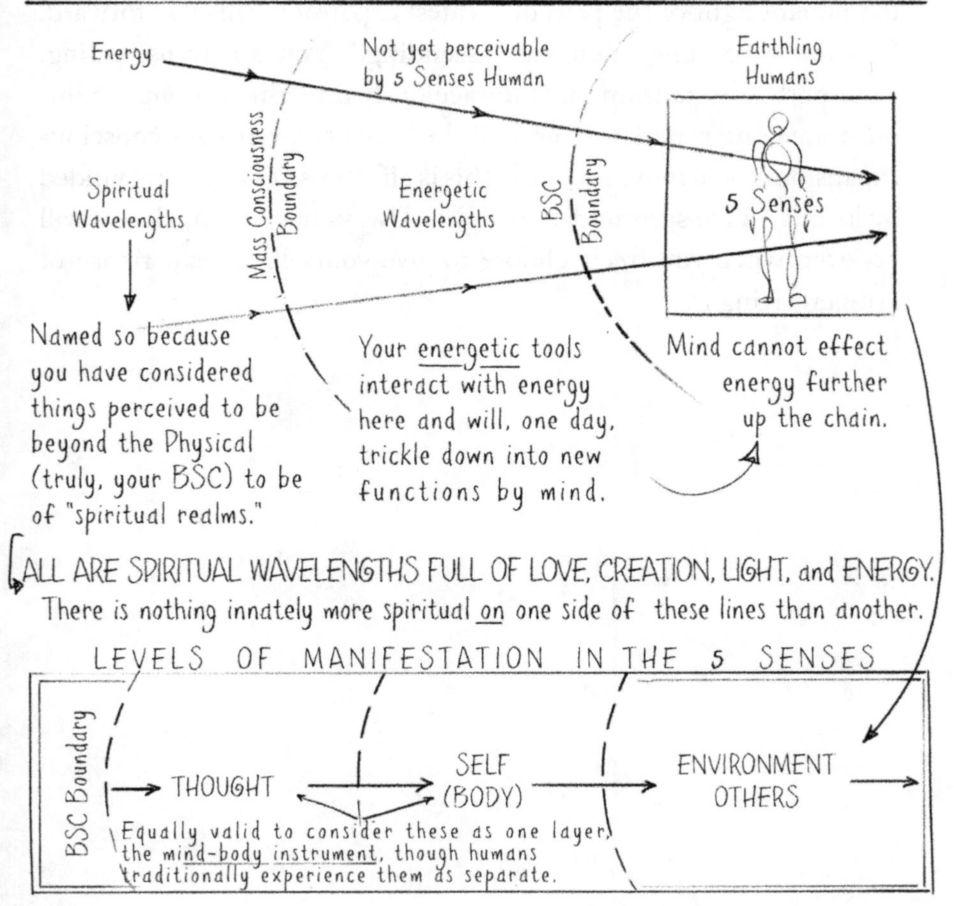

Energy
Not yet perceivable by 5 Senses Human
Earthling Humans
Mass Consciousness Boundary
Spiritual Wavelengths
Energetic Wavelengths
BSC Boundary
5 Senses
Named so because you have considered things perceived to be beyond the Physical (truly, your BSC) to be of "spiritual realms."
Your energetic tools interact with energy here and will, one day, trickle down into new functions by mind.
Mind cannot effect energy further up the chain.
ALL ARE SPIRITUAL WAVELENGTHS FULL OF LOVE, CREATION, LIGHT, and ENERGY.
There is nothing innately more spiritual on one side of these lines than another.
LEVELS OF MANIFESTATION IN THE 5 SENSES
BSC Boundary
THOUGHT
SELF (BODY)
ENVIRONMENT OTHERS
Equally valid to consider these as one layer, the mind-body instrument, though humans traditionally experience them as separate.

Of note:

- The way you perceive self, environment, & others are all manifested after those perceptions have already been molded by, passed through, beliefs.
- Thought could be considered the 1st level of manifestation. It is inside the BSC, thus subject to rules of limitation. This is often why thoughts are difficult to change.
- ESP, clairvoyance, etc, are at "thought" level. Though reflecting expansion, and permeability of this "boundary," they still manifest in thought form.
- Intuition, inspiration, and desire, being energetic perceptions, are thus more expanded than thought, but often rapidly translated to thought, or not consciously recognized by a 5 Senses Human until manifested as a thought (e.g. Sense of Pure Desire vs "I want new shoes").

Illustration 11: Manifestation

Remember, Beloved, your consciousness is expanding because the radiant light of the path of greatest expansion calls you forward. You are expanding. You are "ascending." You are transcending. Your path of expansion most miraculously brought you *through* this most amazing experience, and all the benefits await your conscious expansion as you move forward. This is effortless. You are surrounded by love. You are surrounded by light. Always have been, always will be, even when you freely choose to give yourself the experience of not perceiving it.

Part 2

What You Are Experiencing

We think you are getting the hang of these concepts. Let us review:

Your **resonance** with the **frequency** of disallowance created this experience.

The chief result being your vast, incredible **Belief System Complex (BSC)** and all resulting constructs. Among them: **finiteness, insufficiency, time, distance, body, prevention, and protection.**

This narrowed your perception of energies – your consciousness – to the 5 Senses Spectrum and manifestations on those wavelengths. Which is why we call this Belief System Complex the 5 Senses BSC (the point from which you are perceiving us).

The **path of greatest expansion** led you here, led you through these experiences, and now is leading you beyond them to an expanded perception of new frequencies. This is what we call **transcendence.**

Evidence of your transcendence – which is already underway – can be found in manifestations that exist partially outside the bounds of conscious physicality, such as **imagination** and **memory.**

Your own **perception** of how you shift among frequencies is what you call **emotions.**

Your growing **preference** for **positive emotions,** and more specifically for **love,** is an indication that your path of greatest expansion calls you forward, beyond these frequencies of limitation. As love is the first frequency beyond this massive system of limitation. **For love is your name for the feeling of the momentary cessation of participation in this BSC,** in this frequency of disallowance.

The only concept we have left out of this summation is your Core Frequency – your unique-in-all-creation energetic signature, which radiates purely beyond (or underneath, depending on how you look at it) the layers of beliefs that you have manifested here. This unbreakable connection to the source of all life is how you create. Energy pours through you infinitely and creates perfectly, for whichever frequency with which you have freely chosen to resonate.

Earlier, our Beloved Ones, we asked an important question. Is your emotional array a manifestation of this frequency of limitation you chose to experience? Or is it something more?

We rejoice to be able to tell you that your emotions are perhaps the purest reflection of your Core Frequency in this experience. Even here, as the energy is molded through some many billions of galaxies' worth of belief systems, you still have your own navigational system, your own perception, of the differences in these vast energies that are communicated to you *all the time.*

You can dull them, you can ignore them, you can be unaware of them, but emotions are yours. They are a part of you. And even here, amidst such great limitation, you still cannot undo or prevent your ability to perceive differences in energy, which is fundamental to who you are.

CORE EMOTIONS

The emotional array supercedes belief systems.
Belief systems are manifestations of energy that have already passed through you by way of your existence.

- All life receives energetic frequencies.
- There are different ways of experiencing this energy.
- The Emotional Array way of experienciry energy is unique to your Kind.

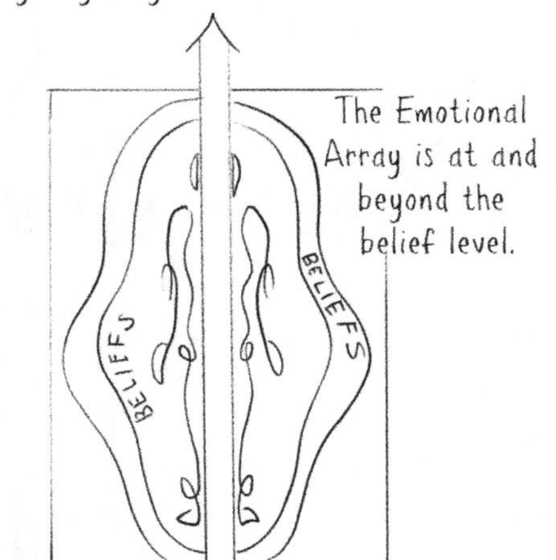

The Emotional Array is at and beyond the belief level.
BELIEFS
BELIEFS

It is difficult for humans to imagine other ways of experiencing energy (e.g. life without emotions?) because, by your conscious recollection, you have perceived none.

Those that radiate in proximity to your CORE FREQUENCY are of like kind, yet you are each still unique! In ways that the limits of mental capacity cannot fathom.

Here, there is a "HUMAN" FREQUENCY or neighborhood of frequencies. This is a continuum.

Where do you draw the line about which is human and which is not?

Illustration 12: Core Emotions

Chapter 6

Energetic Perception

The limits of your squeaks and whistles – that is, human language – make descriptions from here on out a little tricky to manage. You are *just* coming to the perception of these things, thus the energy has not yet trickled all the way down to the specific sound to match. Therefore, going forward, we will be appealing a little more to your energetic perception of our concepts than your mind's perception of them.

Whatever do we mean by that? Let us explain.

We are energy. And you are energy. Your BSC is a fluid, dynamic bundle of energy. The frequency(ies) with which you choose to resonate are energy. Smells are energy too. One word – energy – for a lot of different manifestations, concepts, or experiences, yes?

Let us try to describe to you just *how* different these things are, and the vastness of what remains to be perceived may become more clear to you. We will begin with the easy stuff, which is the energy you already perceive.

The Five Senses

At this point in your timeline, humanity is well aware that your senses perceive energy. You have given names to the wavelengths for each kind of energy – for example, that which the ears receive, and that which the eyes receive. You have found some good concepts as to the atomic structure of what is actually being received by these senses. And you have begun to realize that there are frequencies that exist outside your sensory perception, such as very low sounds that elephants and dogs hear but humans do not. Or light on the infrared spectrum, which insects perceive but human eyes do not.

These have all been important manifestations reflecting your growing awareness of broader frequencies.

As we mentioned before, from our perspective, your mind-body is actually one instrument, tuned to interact with the specific – very narrow – frequencies of this limiting experience. As your Belief System Complex (BSC) compels you to do, you have broken that down further and have named subsections of your complete instrument. You have labeled physical locations in the body as the point of reception of these energies, and moreover the point responsible for specific jobs.

We would like to suggest to you that a great deal more of your mind-body instrument participates in the perception of these energies than the eyeball, the eardrum, and the tongue. Oh, our Beloved Ones, how you make us laugh! That you have this entire instrument, full of fascinating and dynamic collaboration, but you have spent so much of your time separating out and focusing on the eyeball! How completely, how gloriously limiting what you have built here has been! "You have missed the forest for the tree," as your saying goes. Or, as we might say, you have missed the galaxy for the grain of sand.

Let us take each of your senses in turn, and rather than discuss the physical manifestations you believe you perceive via these instrument subsections, we will instead provide an energetic definition of these wavelengths.

Sound

The perception of peripheral frequencies. Sound is your best indicator of energies by which you are surrounded. Your attention to particular sounds will cause you to resonate with them further.

Example: You overhear an intense conversation in a coffee shop but move tables to be out of earshot or put on headphones – this is reflective of your choice of other frequencies. Or, your mind continues to be drawn into the stressful conversation, and after many minutes pass you find that you yourself are feeling tense. You have aligned to the frequency of that conversation.

Sight

The perception of the next frequency. Sight is your best indicator of the frequency you are about to resonate with completely.

Example: When you are driving on autopilot, your eyes continue to move between cars and the road, managing the incoming physical manifestations perfectly. This is the ability of your eyes – your mind-body instrument – to continue to align to the frequency of your next, imminent wavelength even without your conscious management.

Example: This is why people often stare off into the distance when they daydream. The day dreamer has expanded to a broader frequency, and the eyes look at the horizon, or a distance, as a reflection of that breadth.

Smell and Taste

The perception of nuance in a given frequency with which you are resonating.

Example: Someone says, "What's that smell?" And another replies, "I don't smell anything?" Then a minute passes, and the person says, "Wait, now I smell it." In the former case, the person was not yet resonating on that frequency, in the latter they are.

The nuance you perceive with smell and taste is just the beginning of the sensitivity you will begin to develop for energetic frequencies, which will surpass, for quite some time, your ability to describe them with words.

Touch

The perception of real-time energy. When you touch an object or being you are sharing in its present resonance.

Combined, these senses are and have been *just enough* to manage the physical manifestations on these wavelengths of limitation (or perhaps an individual is "missing" a sense, which is an even more powerful contrast). You can see just far enough to perceive danger coming, or food you are hunting. You can smell and taste enough nuance that you know when something is rotten, even if it looks alright. You can hear a variety of things that surround you, any one of which you may freely choose to prevent and thus energize and experience the limitation.

Looking at our list above, you could loosely bunch them into two categories:

- Sound and Sight: the manifestations of **imminent frequencies** that you are heading toward.
- Smell, Taste, and Touch: the manifestations of **real-time frequencies** with which you are aligned.

Yet so small is the difference between the real-time frequencies and the imminent frequencies that, from our vantage point, all of your senses are quite simply the manifested "flavors," if you will, of frequencies with which you are currently aligned.

For example, you see someone's fist in the air, flying toward your face (sight: imminent). You feel the pound of someone's fist connecting with your face (touch: real-time). In that instance, it is a pretty slim margin of separation! And much – though not all – of your perception is like this. Figuratively speaking, you get punched in the face all the time in the 5 Senses BSC!

You are *surprised* all of the time in this BSC. You do not know what is happening just outside of your sensory perception. If someone leaves the room, or drives to the store, you don't know what they are doing. If someone turns off the light in a dark room, you don't know what's going on. Someone can walk back into the room and startle you! You can be hearing all the clicks and whistles in a conversation with others but not truly know what they are thinking. You cannot even see your back sides or your insides! There is so much that is hidden from you. But not for much longer.

The Mind

If you felt like something was missing, or not quite complete, in our energetic description of your 5 senses, you would be correct. We have not yet factored in the mind.

The "mind" is what you call the way, or the place, that you receive the first level of conscious manifestation in the 5 Senses BSC, and that is thought (after which come the manifestations of Self, and the manifestations of Environment). However, is the mind – this receiver of thought – a manifestation as well, or a core part of your structure, like emotion?

From our vantage point, what you are striving to understand here could be considered both.

Earlier we described how the mind is an integral part of your mind-body instrument, which you use to navigate, to experience, this frequency of limitation and disallowance. We also pointed out that the mind aligns to the current barrier of your Consciousness. You are not often consciously aware of the things that the mind does not perceive. You often feel things you are not conscious of. You *believe* things (billions of times per second) that you are not conscious of – yet they are there, they are happening.

Beloved Ones, what you call **the mind is actually the *conscious* embodiment of the frequency of limitation with which you resonated for this experience.** It is the name you have given your consciousness here, when you are limited in the 5 Senses BSC.

You chose, by coming here, to limit your conscious perception of energies to what came through the 5 senses, through the mind-body instrument. But even more importantly, your consciousness, your Mind, is the connection between these sensory stimuli and the

MIND-BODY

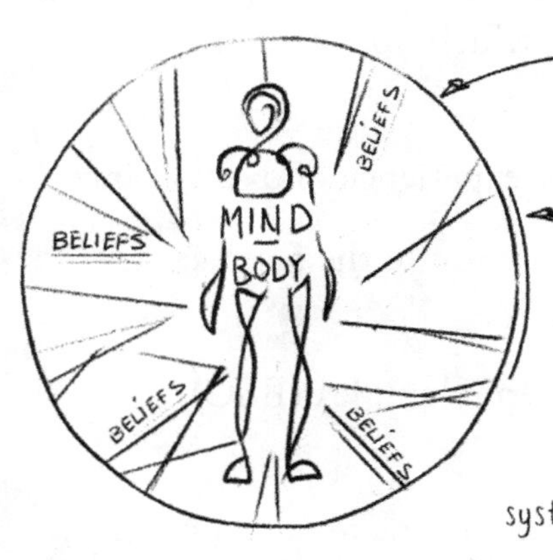
BELIEFS
BELIEFS
BELIEFS
BELIEFS
MIND
BODY

The massive Belief System Complex, where, from our vantage point, mind and body are one, unified system.

Human consciousness had overlapped completely with this system, but now it is expanding.

This is why humans cannot yet make choices on an infinite scale - human consciousness has overlapped with a system designed to not think about the infinite.

THE FUNCTION OF THE BSC/MIND:

Collection of limiting beliefs that narrow the human perception of existence to what is perceived by the 5 Senses (thus disallowing the perception of the infinite). Choices are made based upon beliefs that analyze, prioritize, dismiss, or validate the 5 Senses perceptions.

5 SENSES BSC PROCESS

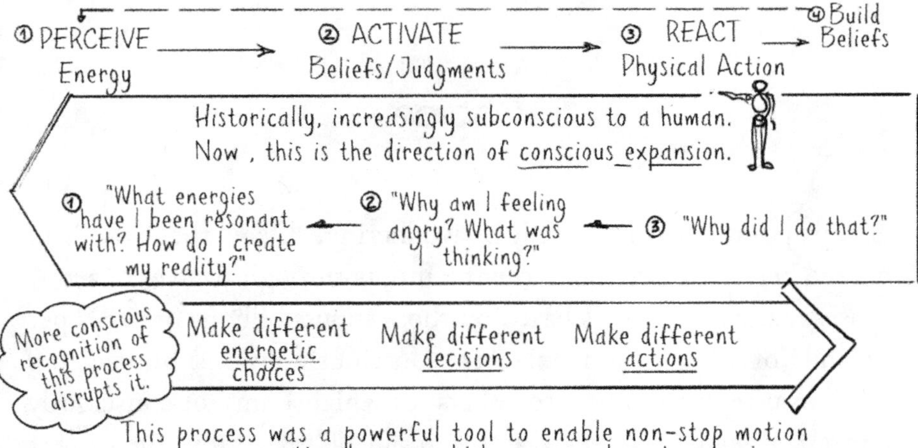
① PERCEIVE
Energy
② ACTIVATE
Beliefs/Judgments
③ REACT
Physical Action
④ Build Beliefs
Historically, increasingly subconscious to a human.
Now, this is the direction of conscious expansion.
① "What energies have I been resonant with? How do I create my reality?"
② "Why am I feeling angry? What was I thinking?"
③ "Why did I do that?"
More conscious recognition of this process disrupts it.
Make different energetic choices
Make different decisions
Make different actions

This process was a powerful tool to enable non-stop motion across your emotional array, which you came here to experience directly, specifically.

Mind is capable of receiving wavelengths beyond the 5 Senses. As you expand, so does your physical manifestation, including Mind.

Illustration 13: Mind-Body

vast ocean of beliefs in your BSC, which dictates the majority of your actions, choices, and experiences here. This setup drives you through experiences of disallowance, which you perceive by your emotional array.

Thus both of these facets create the experience of disallowance:

- The *limitation* of conscious perception to the 5 senses stimuli (core part of your being)
- The *connection* to the Belief System Complex (BSC) (manifestation)

Together, these two critical functions make up your entire "reality." And you have chosen to call these functions – this location – your mind.

The current limitation of your consciousness, no matter what you call it, and its connection to the vast Belief System Complex (BSC), is the lynchpin of this entire experience.

Choice

At this point, you may rightly be wondering, "Okay, then who is in charge here? If I am only receiving inputs through five very narrow senses, activating beliefs based on those inputs billions of times per second (of which I am not even consciously aware!) and feeling disallowance based on those beliefs (of which I am not consciously aware!), then I am likely reacting to all of that. How then can I possibly make decisions? How do I have choice in these things? Or are my decisions driven by this whole setup?"

You sense rightly, Beloved, how incredibly vast this system of limitation has been!

And, indeed, before we answer your question, we must describe this limitation even further.

This setup not only affects your outputs – meaning the actions you choose to make based on what you perceive and believe – it actually affects the inputs themselves.

If you do not *believe* something is possible, you will not perceive it.

If the *collective*, meaning the consensus of participants in the BSC, does not allow for something to be perceived, you will not perceive it.

This is part of the rules of engagement in this game. And you wanted this! Wanted this profound, complete, amazing experience of immense limitation!

Thus, you may be standing in front of a being who is partially outside the rules of your game, and you will not see it, hear it, smell it, or touch it. There may be methods to circumvent time, heal your limited body, or span great distances, but you will not conceive of it. Not until your experience here is complete.

And how do you know when it is complete?

Beloved, before you came here, you did not exist in a concept of time. You did not say, I will go into this experience of limitation for 1 million years, and then I will be done. Instead, you vibrated from a place of pure love and expanded into this frequency in radiant trust. You *knew* that the light of creation would move you through this frequency, the way it always does. You *knew* that eventually you would expand beyond and because of this experience, too. You knew that the "time" you spent here would be perfect, *just the right amount*, for your greatest expansion.

You will see, Beloved Ones, you will see – as you expand just a little further, just a little broader, that the clarity will begin to flow to you of just how effortlessly perfect this all has been. And you will feel a deep and resonant bliss that has been as-yet untold of in your kind.

This vast BSC influences both what you are capable of perceiving – even within the spectra of your 5 senses – as well as how you are capable of responding. In a sense, the BSC is the framework for a limited set of acceptable responses in order to play the game. This dictation of "right action" has been unconscious to you. Thus, you feel like each conversation is a little different, or each day is a little different – and in truth, they are, for even here the expansiveness of creation cannot be completely limited. Yet, from a broader perspective these actions have been wholly constrained.

Do you know how many arguments you have had with others over the finiteness of creation – land, money, food, rights, stuff?

Do you know how long you have been trying to get off the same "planet"?

How many thousands of years you have obsessed over clothes, your appearance, the shape of your eyes, or the length of your nails?

How many times you have born children?

How many times you have lost things?

Oh, our Beloved Ones, billions upon billions of years!

Viewed from this perspective, this experience has been completely limiting! Completely… redundant.

And what a powerful concept this is, for redundancy is a belief of *this* BSC. Only here can things happen again and again in relatively the same way. Only here could you do something "too much" that wasn't really needed, or turn a crank too far, or have two people accidentally make the same thing! Only here could *any action, any creation, any choice* be considered other than what it is – a purely unique, divine creation of all that is. It is *by your beliefs* that you think things are limited, and you manifest evidence of this. And it is *by your beliefs* that you believe *anything could be done in error.*

Cycles

Perhaps now you understand, Beloved Ones, how repetition, redundancy, and error occur here, because you believe it to be possible, wholly and unconsciously.

This is the origin of your concepts of the karmic wheel, and the great repeating patterns of life and the universe. It is because you believed it to be so in order to create this experience of limitation.

The BSC limits what you perceive, you activate beliefs based on these limited perceptions, you feel the variety of emotions that reflect your disallowance of energies, and you take action based upon a framework of acceptable responses.

When you feel ashamed, can you disappear into the Earth? Nope. Can you rocket to a different dimension? Nope. Can you go just slightly backwards in time and adjust what you might have said? Nope. You can say something, say nothing, or leave (and maybe a few other choices beyond that).

Thus this experience – with only the slightest of modifications – repeats, repeats, repeats. As you disallow, disallow, disallow.

And perhaps most critical of all is the final piece of this masterpiece you have built – **new beliefs are built, billions of times per second, based on what is *manifested.***

"But wait!" you say. "I thought what is manifested was limited by beliefs?" Yes, to both, Beloved. It is a two-way game. Your beliefs limit what is manifested, or what about that manifestation can be perceived. *And* you build beliefs based upon that limited perception. It is, one might say, an endless cycle.

This is what you agreed to by coming here. To enmesh yourself in the BSC, drastically limit your conscious perception to the 5 senses, and to build beliefs – that is, contribute to the game – based upon this limited perception of the universe. Thus, things become more true, more true, and more true, until it is nearly impossible for any exception, *any new energy*, to make it all the way down to the wavelengths of the 5 senses.

Now you know, Beloved. Now you know why this experience that you have built has not only been so very fascinating to all of us who have been able to perceive your experience of it but also has been an unprecedented example of the glory of creation. That is why so many are here, *right now*, to see how this all plays out.

You vibrated wholly and purely with this frequency of disallowance, trusting the path of greatest expansion to bring you forward. And here you created a complete cycle of limitation – where not only are you limited in what you perceive, but what you perceive furthers the limitation – over and over and over again. And, after billions of years, the colossal machine you have built is both profound and impenetrable.

But then ... you began daydreaming. And then, you began to prefer positive emotions. And then, you found names for them, and you named love. And you began to celebrate it. And now, you are awakening to all that you are beyond this game!

That the light of creation would bring you through these wavelengths was never in doubt. But the "how," as you might call it, is a blessed mystery that we revel in watching unfold. And one that, by being able to share in your experience here, causes us all to understand more deeply, and to resonate more expansively, with the light and love of all creation.

CYCLES

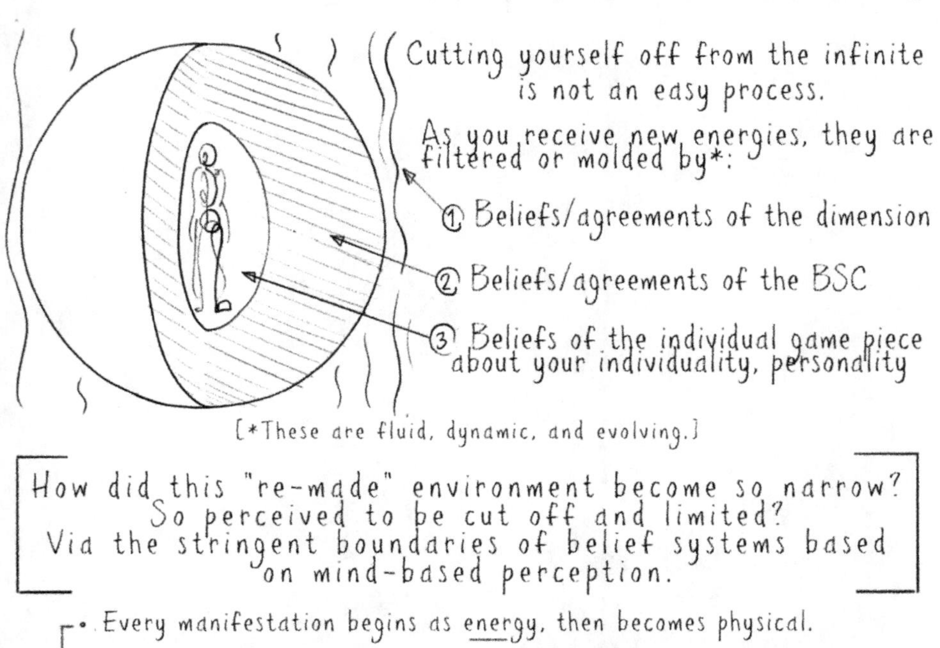

Cutting yourself off from the infinite is not an easy process.
As you receive new energies, they are filtered or molded by*:
① Beliefs/agreements of the dimension
② Beliefs/agreements of the BSC
③ Beliefs of the individual game piece about your individuality, personality
[*These are fluid, dynamic, and evolving.]
How did this "re-made" environment become so narrow? So perceived to be cut off and limited? Via the stringent boundaries of belief systems based on mind-based perception.

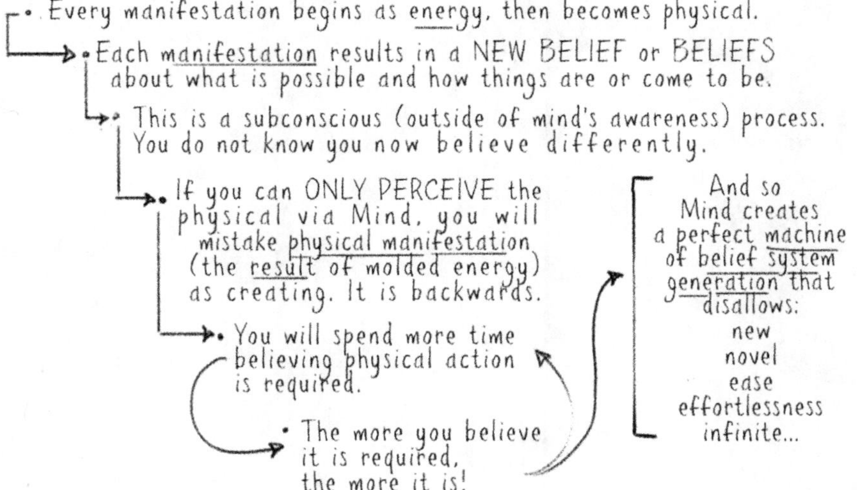

• Every manifestation begins as energy, then becomes physical.
• Each manifestation results in a NEW BELIEF or BELIEFS about what is possible and how things are or come to be.
• This is a subconscious (outside of mind's awareness) process. You do not know you now believe differently.
• If you can ONLY PERCEIVE the physical via Mind, you will mistake physical manifestation (the result of molded energy) as creating. It is backwards.
• You will spend more time believing physical action is required.
• The more you believe it is required, the more it is!
And so Mind creates a perfect machine of belief system generation that disallows:
new
novel
ease
effortlessness
infinite...

How does this feel? Via your beliefs of LACK, you DISALLOW and thus experience the FULL emotional array.

THIS IS WHAT YOU CAME HERE TO KNOW.

Illustration 14: Cycles

Chapter 7

Energetic Loopholes

This book is a manifestation. All the words and concepts thus far are a manifestation. And, Beloved, you have, all along – billions of times per second – been writing new beliefs based on this manifestation with every page you turned.

But how, you might ask, did this make it through the machine? And namely, *your machine*, of all the beliefs you agreed to broadly, and all of your individual beliefs as well?

Humans do believe in loopholes, do you not? How on Earth did *that* belief make it through? A small enough of a crack in the facade that something *slightly* different could work its way in. The beginning of a new path to the beyond that would grow.

The new energy of expanded consciousness comes through subtly at first, as something just slightly different from what has already been allowed in, but that manifestation is enough. You build a belief about the "possibility" of something different, which allows in something slightly different again, and so on.

It is a gradual, slow process, you might say. From another, equally valid vantage point, it is an incredibly efficient and effective way of expanding beyond such a colossal machine of disallowance.

Possibility

Currently, your conscious idea of "possibility" is your way of defining your current experience, your current perspective.

When you declare something to be possible, what goes unsaid is, "*In my experience*, this is possible, and that is not." Beliefs in possibility span far beyond your individual belief systems into the core of the BSC. Possibility is defined at the aggregate level. Understand that it is a reflection of your vibrational set point, which happens to be here, on the frequency of disallowing. Possibility is completely changeable. **If you are capable of achieving an infinite number of perspectives, or frequencies, then truly infinite things are possible.**

You might be surprised to find that the idea of possibility – or rather, that some things are not possible – is actually one of your greatest loopholes.

Let us pretend, for a moment, that you had a belief, which manifested as an event. As a result of that event, you believe that a thing (we will call Thing A) is not possible. In goes the belief to the BSC: "Thing A, not possible." It ripples through the complex and is rapidly adopted by all players. "Copy that. Thing A, not possible." This will affect all future manifestations of Thing A across the game board.

But there is a hiccup in the matrix. Because now, "Thing A" is coded into the vastness of the BSC itself, accessible by all players. In the negation of the Thing, you have actually recorded the essence of it.

(Beloved, this is not the last time that you will find a humorous analogy for your experiences of this BSC in your "technology." It is but a reflection of you, yourself, and your energetic experience here.)

Onward goes manifestation, and each time new energy comes in, it is filtered and molded by all the beliefs, down and down and down, including "Thing A, not possible."

Is it possible that another Thing could come along, perhaps millions of years later, that is also not possible? Of course. And let us call that thing, Thing Z3000.

Now, is it equally possible, in a realm of *infinite* possibility that if Thing Z3000 is *not* possible, that this might mean that Thing A from a million years prior, must be? Yes.

Is not this idea perhaps so commonplace to you now as to seem benign? In science, you declare something to be categorically impossible, only to uncover, perhaps even decades later, other discoveries that make the once-impossible thing suddenly plausible. Another example: in your courts, a judgment is made and a precedent is set, only to be overturned years later by courts and judges who find themselves in scenarios the prior judicial teams could have never imagined.

What you find perhaps commonplace now was at one time unmanifested, was at one time un-existent in your reality.

This first instance was nothing less than the collision between the infinite universe of possibility of where you come from, and the limited perception of reality in which you are here immersed.

A radiant burst of light made it all the way down to the 5 Senses levels, and, with the probability of 1 in infinity, collided with what had already been defined before. It was a loophole, buried in a galactic machine of limitation. Though it would be a tall order to expect your limited consciousness to identify it, energetically you could. Something was *possible* that had *not been* before. It was the energy of *different*.

You gave this loophole a name: change.

And then, it was (and is) available to all of you. In that instant, *somewhere* in the BSC, there was both a frequency of Thing A being not possible *and* an instance of Thing A being possible. Therefore, playing by the rules of course, it was possible for this instance, this collision, to trickle all the way down to your consciousness, until one day, out of billions, one among you was able to say, "You all think Thing A is not possible, but I, I think *it is.*"

And the aggregate would *have* to allow that perception through, because it was completely within the rules of the game, completely within the boundaries of the BSC.

Would all members of the BSC need to consciously experience that disagreement? Not at all. In fact, you could have just said it in your heart, or in your mind (the first level of manifestation), and a *new belief* would be written as a result of that manifestation. *It is possible for a Thing that was not possible* to change *and become possible.*

And in that instant you might have heard a heavenly choir sing, "Freedom!" For in this one loophole, you were on your way. It was the very first step, the very first belief of a new BSC.

Change

If you think in probabilities, and you are adding up all the galaxies of beliefs that live to prevent a non-limiting aspect like change through to the playing field versus that one nugget of difference, you might say, "That moment was truly a miracle."

And it was! For **"miracle" is your way of defining a low- to no-possibility outcome based upon the summation of conscious and unconscious beliefs in the BSC.** When witnessing a miracle, consciously you say, "It's not possible!" While unconsciously, your energy is vibrating with, "Somewhere in the sea of possibility that was completely possible, and beliefs of this BSC aligned in a very precise way for this one to slip through." (Or perhaps it was perfectly allowed through, hmm?)

Low probability is not impossibility, even here!

You connected to a frequency that was *just* alongside this frequency of limitation. You expanded almost imperceptibly and caught it perfectly.

It might sound strange to you, consciously, to connect to the idea that at some point *the loophole of change* was established. Meaning, that there were experiences in this BSC that were outside of, or prior to, *change*?

There were, our Beloved Ones.

You are just beginning to connect to how vastly limiting and powerful and perfect this experience has been. Compared to where you have been in this vast complex of limiting beliefs, you are more surrounded by change now than you have ever been. Yet, even so, it is still not as rapidly changing as it is in pure flow (faster than even billions of times per second).

Do you experience a change of seasons planet-wide? Yes, you do. Is it still a cycle of seasons? Yes, it is. For now.

Do you age and change, year by year? Yes, you do. Is it still a path of deterioration? Yes, it is. For now.

Can you change jobs, houses, friends, and pets? You can and do. Does your excitement over those things still wane with time? Yes. Do those things deteriorate as well? Yes. For now.

There is change in your conscious perception – beautiful, glorious, life-giving change – but there is still an underlayer of finiteness and insufficiency. There is both. Because *you are both.*

Beloved, you have one foot in a new, more consciously expanded BSC into which you are growing, *and* you have the other foot still in the existing BSC. For a time, you will experience *both.* You will see – you will perceive with your thoughts, with your senses – experiences of finiteness and insufficiency, as well as enlightenment and expansion.

You will notice the suffering of others and be motivated to prevention and protection. And the next day you may experience a moment of relaxation where you feel, throughout your whole being, that everything, and everyone, is okay and that there is nothing you must do.

You will notice wrinkles and grey hair, and berate yourself for eating cookies. And the next day, you will find that even in the middle of an argument with a co-worker, you realize that you are not really that upset at all. It is like watching someone else say the words coming out of your mouth.

You will feel compelled to stay connected to everything (terrible) that is happening in the world. And then there will be moments where you truly feel like you love everyone. And we mean *everyone.*

CHANGE

Mind does not sense the energetic connection to the next thought or manifestation in the series on the wavelength of that desire. Humans perceive there to be a "gap" between 5 Senses manifestations.

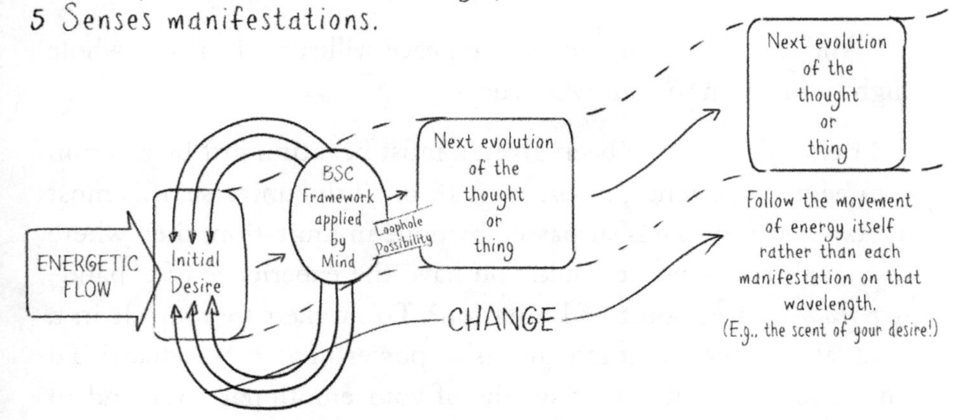

In this "gap," mind works on, or re-makes, the existing idea (manifestation) in order to bring it to fruition. This is why it may seem difficult to let go of the initial idea of a desire.

Like all physical interactions, it is moving the existent physical stuff around (thought/plans included!) in order to get what you want.

The energetic stability that is required to bridge the "gap" is UNCHARACTERISTIC of humankind at this juncture because it was not part of your objective in this domain.

Instead, your objective was the redirection, by the BSC, back to existing physical manifestation as a method to continue to immerse yourself in the emotional array.

Illustration 15: Change

Some days you will have long conversations with your partner about all the things you are worried about. You will go to bed feeling as though you are in the pit of despair and cannot handle the burden of these things any longer. And then, one night, you will be awakened in the wee hours by a feeling of peace that is indescribable.

And, over time, that feeling of peace will spread to your whole nights, and then to your whole days.

Beloved, you have been given a most beautiful gift by creation – to be, to experience, *awakening*. If, in all the universe, this most amazing experience is surpassed by none in limitation, then where else in all the universe could you have the experience of expanding *from* such a point of limitation? To awaken to yourself in a gradual, perfect unfolding that is as powerful as it is radiant? To know, to be, in such vast swaths of your emotional array and to move into conscious choice of these things? And the fun is only just beginning!

Control

Humanity is immersed in a grand illusion. That is, the belief that you could ever be *not* in control. Your own bodies, others, events of nature – you believe that any measure, *any experience* of existence, could possibly be out of control. Conversations, planes, weather systems, toddlers, blenders, ideas, parties, emotions … all of these could very possibly go out of control. Of course.

Because of this fundamental belief, you energize – you activate – limitation. Powerful regions of belief like prevention and protection, which energize manifestations, which would *require or make necessary* your prevention and protection. And thus you become locked in this cycle of which we have been speaking, where your beliefs cause the energization of limitation, which produces limiting manifestations, which causes the building of new, limiting beliefs, and so on. Thus, you exist in perpetual lifetimes where control is lost. You create various methods to assure control, but inevitably things arise that result in a new version of loss of control, and you must create more methods.

This, you recognize within you. This aspect of yourselves you have brought to consciousness.

Now let us look at the relationship between Change and Control.

If change is the harbinger of new life, new energy, and new beliefs to you, then why is it not so easily welcomed? Why is it that you find yourself cringing, or growing a little squeamish, or downright anxious when you sense or perceive a change to your environment, your routines, your homes, your bodies? Why is change so stressful now that you know its energetic quality?

Thus, let us define Control energetically, and it will bring more clarity to how these things interact. Your perception will grow.

Energetically, **control is the reduction of energies into the accepted framework of possibilities** that is the foundation of this BSC. You sense this in the *feeling* of things being well in control. It is the judgment, by mind, of all things aligning to the accepted framework in a way that is conceivable.

See if you can sense for a moment how the feeling of control – of everything in its right place, time, and order – *could* feel like a cousin to the feeling of joy? Do you see, Beloved, how these senses of energy relate to each other? They are on a wavelength of right judgment by mind though of differing degrees. Do not worry if you do not sense this yet.

You have guessed rightly so very often that you are capable of more. Sometimes this comes across as a manifested idea or discovery about the potential within the squishy substrate that you call the brain. Sometimes this is manifested in feats believed physically impossible by the squishy parts of the body you call muscles. But, even then, you still feel like there must be *more*. More that is not yet even reflected in any aspect of your mind-body instrument perceivable on the 5 Senses Spectrum. You seek a sixth sense. Surely there must be another!

There are infinitely more, in fact! But the *sense* of this more is absolutely critical. It is what matters most at this juncture.

This *more* of you does exist, outside the limited perceptions of this BSC. This sense of more is your rendezvous with these frequencies by energetic parts of yourself. These parts, as of yet, have not been named. But they exist and they are real. And these energetic parts will perceive so much more than what you have yet been able to perceive consciously that it will feel as such a vastness as you have never sensed before.

In the coming years and decades, these parts of you will become more and more apparent. Why? Because you will be vibrating into a new BSC that is not *as* limiting as the 5 Senses BSC. Freed from those agreements, you will be able to perceive these broader frequencies, these capabilities you have, because you are no longer limited from doing so. Said another way, it is your most expansive path to become aware of these things.

As this occurs, your beliefs about "control" or "not being in control" will also shift.

Subject to the agreements of this BSC, you believe, both consciously and subconsciously, billions of times per second, that all sorts of things could happen to you that you did not consciously choose, wish for, or allow. You did not choose for that car to hit you. You did not consciously wish for a relationship that would end in divorce. You did not declare that a hailstorm should arrive, let alone damage your roof. So you build stoplights, side mirrors, airbags, and alarm systems and feel a little bit *safer*. You remain alert to subtle changes in your partner's demeanor, you read books on how to maintain healthy relationships, and you feel a little more *confident*. You check the weather, buy insurance, develop tougher roof shingles, and feel a little bit more *prepared*.

These are all sensations of right judgment by mind. They are each versions of control.

Yet, in all of these examples, we must append something important, something critical. And that is – *ahead of time*.

Time, yet again, structures your perception of your own reality in a way you do not concretely sense.

We understand that a human would say, "Look, you're telling me that energetically I was heading toward a hailstorm. But *I* didn't know that, so I couldn't *change my path*, my frequency, to avoid the hailstorm that I didn't want."

In this case, there is the critical concept of moments before the hailstorm, when conscious recognition was not made, when action could not have been taken, where the impending thing to avoid was still impending, yes?

How would you take this same example *without* the concept of time?

Let us help.

"I am perfection. All things flow through me."

Sound a little too nebulous for your liking? Just give us time! Ha!

In this glorious point of flowing you perceive, you conceive of, all of your infinite choices. You would see the possibility of being under that hailstorm *as equally as possible* as not being in that hailstorm. Time would be irrelevant. It would have no bearing on your ability to know or even to choose the experience of that hailstorm. You do not require a moment *before* the hailstorm in order to *avoid* the hailstorm.

When you feel as though you are not in control, did not consciously choose this change, or any change – understand that you are simply perceiving new energy by way of the 5 Senses BSC. Which would tell you that in order to be in control, there must be:

1. A moment in time, before said manifestation, where the conscious mind names, defines, and desires said manifestation

2. A matching manifestation

If either of these conditions is not met, or only partially met, there is a *conscious sense of lack of control.* And in bringing that to consciousness, you activate, energize, and create additional beliefs about *not being in control!*

As you may be realizing, you created a limited ability to perceive much of anything, so how often do you think you meet criteria #1 above? You're right, not often.

But then, life continues to "surprise" you, doesn't it? So even if you were able to name – in advance – specifically what you want to manifest, how often does life *identically match* that conception? You're right, not often.

Thus, how often do you think you are building beliefs – and matching manifestations – about *not* being in control?

All. The. Time.

"That car cut in front of me." *Not in control.*

"You said you'd make that reservation but you forgot!" *Not in control.*

"Oh, no. I didn't mean to break that." *Not in control.*

"And then she got really angry and yelled at everyone." *Not in control.*

If mind has a *preconceived* notion of how a manifestation will – or should! – take place, take to heart, Beloved Ones, that this manifestation – the thought – has just built a belief.

And that belief has just activated limitation.

And that limitation molds the energy from what it *would have been* – novel, creative, powerful – into something *accepted by your BSC framework.*

You receive the sense of a desire. And almost instantaneously your mind says, "Shoes! I want those shoes! A white pair of shoes just like that." And like a ping pong ball on a floor full of mouse-traps a galaxy wide, beliefs are activated about the possibility of getting those shoes – have you seen them before, are they in your price range, do you have that money, do you have time to get them, do you deserve them, do you have shoes that are already too much like them…

And the energy of that pure desire that lasted *but a fraction of a moment* before it became shoes, is molded, molded, molded, molded into something almost identical to all the shoes which have come before.

And the matching sensation is what you call "control."

CONTROL

① Desire originates from your largest self, from the furthest edge of yourself.

② Here, only here, do you not perceive this part of yourself, and so it may feel like you are "not in control" - that another part of you is deciding your existence here and what you feel "called to."

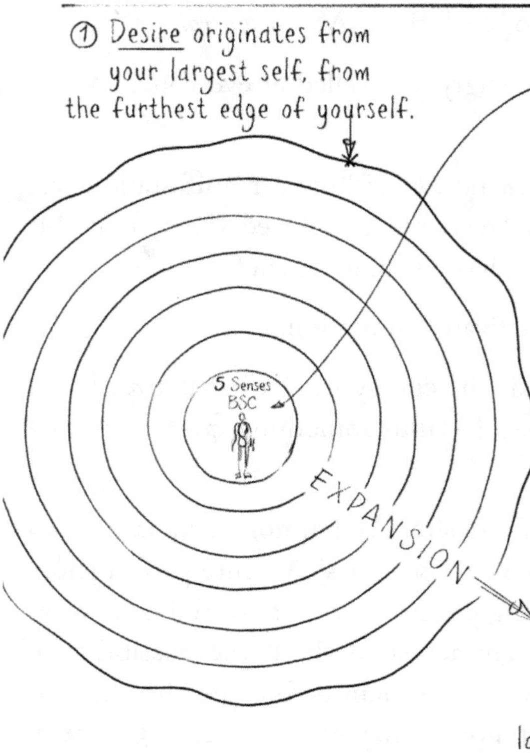

③ But understand this was part of the [creation] of feeling [out of] control. A perspective of this. A perception of this.

④ And now you are beginning to recollect these things. You are releasing feelings of lack of control - because you are experiencing a conscious AWAKENING - a reconnection of the mental consciousness to all aspects of what and who you are.

⑤ Said another way, you are GAINING senses of control, choice, empowerment, security, safety, freedom...

You created this BSC in a perfect unfolding of limitation, which was on your most expansive path.

⑥ You were never not in control.

Illustration 16: Control

Chapter 8

Energetic Flow

The *energy of change* is that pure moment – that split second – of desire before it is adapted by the BSC. The activation of beliefs about what is an acceptable desire within the framework is so immediate that you have historically not been able to sense the gap between this pure moment and the thought itself.

In fact, your language has this structure. You must say I desire *something*. You do not say, "I desire." You do not wander around your house shouting, "I desire! I desire! I desire!" Your family would shout back, "Get on with it! Go get what you desire so we don't have to listen to you anymore!"

So, it would seem, if you are keen to transcend consciously, we have a bit of a conundrum. If you cannot stop the activation of your own BSC, then how can you allow the energy of change to come through to you *without* being molded, molded, molded into what is limiting and insufficient?

How do you *consciously* choose the frequency of the New BSC if, by virtue of your present overlap between both BSCs, your consciousness is – activates – the limitation of the 5 Senses BSC?

Action

Let us pause here and review the options at hand.

- 5 Senses BSC: You could take some sort of conscious action to modify your participation in the BSC.
- New BSC: You could consciously make an energetic shift.

Let us address the former, first.

You live in a realm of "do." For every thought, every new idea, every desire that comes through to you, colossal mountains of belief are activated that tell you that you must take some sort of action on the 5 Senses Spectrum to assist in bringing that idea or desire into your reality.

This is our definition of **action: the instantaneous identification that an idea or desire has not yet been manifested on the 5 Senses Spectrum, and the activation of beliefs within the framework that dictate acceptable expenditures of energy in response to that identification of lack.**

That was a mouthful! Let's break that down a little bit.

Let's begin by looking at just the first part of our definition: the instantaneous identification that an idea or desire has not yet manifested on the 5 Senses Spectrum (e.g., I want those shoes, and I do not already own them).

This is what we call the Intersection of Do – it is the collision of a conscious perception of desire with the conscious perception that the desire has not *yet* been met. Again, your concept of time is the backbone to this structure.

You have probably felt this intersection numerous times already while reading this book. This new information causes a launching of new desires, which you recognize as not yet being resolved, and so you ask, "But what do I *do*?"

You are now conscious of your 5 Senses Belief System Complex. You are conscious of the New BSC you are building. You would like to expand into that New BSC. And so, without your conscious say-so, all the beliefs activate and cause you to say or think, "But how do I get there? How do I do that?"

And in the asking of that question, you have reinforced limitation, because it is based upon your recognition that your desire has not yet been met. Otherwise, why would there be anything *to do?* If you felt that the New BSC is inevitable, if you felt like it would be fundamentally impossible for you to mess it up, if you believed all sorts of different things than are active in this 5 Senses BSC, would you even ask what you needed to do? Or would you already be reveling in the new manifestation?

Thus, Beloved, reflect on all the times in your days, your years, your lifetimes, in which you have felt you needed to do something. Make dinner, pick up your kids, vote, pay a bill, buy groceries, talk to someone … every single one of those actions had been instigated by the recognition of a desire that had not yet been met! And every time you *take those actions*, you are energizing the frequency of their not being met.

How beautifully, fantastically, completely limiting! Do you see how the entire existence of a human in the 5 Senses BSC activates, builds, and contributes to, over and over and over again, the concepts of finiteness and insufficiency? The pure, bold limitation of it all!

Think on this: how many to-do lists, requirements, documents, strategies, and any sort of plan through all the centuries have all been energizing the frequency of desires *not yet being met?* You arrange entire careers over the achievement of milestones that have not yet been met! So fundamental to your existence here is planning and doing, that you are not even sure how else it might be possible to exist!

But let us go even further into the Intersection of Do, by examining the latter half of our definition of action: the activation of beliefs within the framework that dictate acceptable expenditures of energy in response to that identification of lack (e.g., I want those shoes, I do not already own them. *Pulls out phone to begin searching on the internet for them*).

So far we have seen the collision of a desire with the recognition that it has not yet come to pass, and now we see a third collision: the activation of all of the beliefs in acceptable ways to expend your energy – to do – within the framework. These, also, are limited.

As we have said before, can you build a house in a minute while it takes an average person in the BSC a year? Nope.

Thus you redouble your energization of the limitation of the BSC by manifesting – by way of your own limited action – a reinforcement of a select few ways to respond. When those limited ways of taking action do not quickly result in the original desire, you build more beliefs about the difficulty of achieving the things you desire.

Beloved, the system of limitation you built here is practically watertight. Thus, it is so beautiful, so miraculous, so wonderful that you have been able to receive, to perceive, the energy of change.

ACTION

There are many beliefs about Physical Control that re-capture energy into pre-existent manifestations.
Like, CONSISTENCY...
By believing you must re-do, re-do, re-do, re-do, re-do, re-do the same action to get the desired result, you spend large amounts of your time:

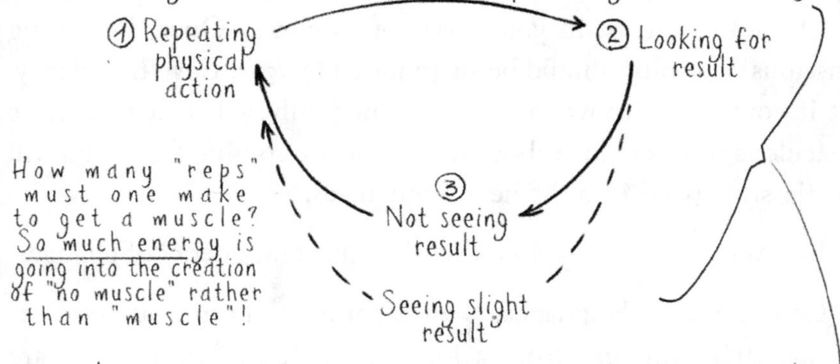

① Repeating physical action
② Looking for result
③ Not seeing result
Seeing slight result
How many "reps" must one make to get a muscle? So much energy is going into the creation of "no muscle" rather than "muscle"!

EACH of the steps in this cycle re-energizes existent manifestation/conditions, until...
A certain amount of time/effort passes that you believe (often unconsciously!) is sufficient.
This momentary allowance releases the energy into the creation of "new," which often includes a fraction of the desired result.

Some have noticed if you bypass steps 2 and 3 (e.g., don't think about it, just keep going to workout), you can accelerate the time to result or at least achieve it.

This may be because you are spending less energy activating mind's beliefs and judgments over the presence/progress of results.
Hovever, you are still fundamentally participating in the cycle, even if it is a narrower loop
narrower loop
narrower loop
narrower loop...

Illustration 17: Action

Inspiration

So what now? You may feel distrusting of your own ideas for action, knowing how they typically are taken from a stance of needing to achieve, or make happen, that which you desire.

Do not lose trust in yourselves, our Beloved Ones. Becoming conscious of a thing should be surrounded by *love*. Love this clarity. Let it continue to flow to you. And not only will you find more miraculous things to love about where you are coming from, you will effortlessly expand into the next frequencies.

Let us continue to explore this all-important energy of change.

Often, in your languages, change connotes a physical manifestation that is different from a long succession of things that are similar. In fact, the longer a thing has remained similar, the greater this change can feel.

Yet, you now know that when we talk about the meaning of change energetically, ours is tied to the idea of possibility. Energetically, there are now two equally possible paths, and your perception of that possibility, that freedom of choice, is change.

In the former case, it is by your comparison of the "change" to everything that came before that you reinstate the limitation. For example, you do not choose a new home without a great deal of analysis and activity by mind: a great deal of judgments and beliefs that are activated. In this flurry of activity, you assess all the things about your current home that you like and don't like, and then apply that rubric to the evaluation of future homes, the selection of the home, and the moving into the new home. In a sense, you continually slow everything down by your constant activation of the belief systems of mind over every detail, every aspect of the choice – of the change you are making. And, as you well know, the rollercoaster of emotions most people feel through this process is their perception of a variety of flavors of disallowing!

This activity – this analysis – is *not* fundamental to the energy of change, though, is it? You see this now. The energy of change was that moment of pure desire where you realized – somehow, some way – that you *wanted* a *new* something, and then that frequency was molded into something acceptable, which was the home.

That beautiful, refreshing, exciting, life-giving desire is the energy of change. All the negative emotions you connote with change are actually just more examples of your beautiful, perfect, impressive system of disallowance.

Every thought that followed that first concept of "new house" in your bringing to fruition that new house is a molding of energy within the boundaries of the 5 Senses BSC.

Could you have done it any other way?

Yes, you could and can. Because you have access to a new and growing body of beliefs of the New BSC.

Energetically this will be much easier for you, for now. This is because the mind – as we have mentioned – is currently enmeshed in agreements. All your "thinking" is heavily bound by the rules of the game, strongly connected to the oceans of beliefs that are activated consciously and unconsciously by all the 5 Senses stimuli you receive. Your expanding consciousness, however – where you find your imagination, your memories – can play the game a little more loosely.

Thus, we will discuss an alternate path that is a way of experiencing these processes energetically and by doing so vibrating at a slightly different frequency than the 5 Senses BSC.

Let us begin by discussing another energetic perception you already have available to you, and that is inspiration.

You have identified this frequency and well understand what it means. An inspiration is more flexible in both time and beliefs than any of your rational, logical thoughts. Why is this? Because it is the perception of energies slightly beyond, or next to, the agreements of the BSC. As such, it can be of a moment – meaning, an inspiration does not have to connect or relate to what is currently happening on the linear timeline. It can also be what one might consider irrational, illogical, silly, or nonsensical, because it is slightly outside the bounds of acceptable (limited) thinking. (Of course, once it is judged to be so, the energy is being modified, and it will be molded into something acceptable.)

You might be cooking dinner and suddenly feel inspired to book a trip to Mexico. The trip could be completely unrelated to the food you are cooking or what is going on in the room. The trip may also be a nonsensical cost, or poorly timed. Yet, you can still perceive the inspiration.

You might be having a conversation with a friend when you suddenly feel inspired to get up and go outside. These sorts of inspirations are often very instantly counteracted by your conscious beliefs about social protocol. It would be considered rude to get up in the middle of a conversation!

Though you may often choose not to act on them, you are still perceiving inspiration more frequently.

Moreover, and perhaps most especially, inspiration does not violate a sense of control, does it? Earlier when we spoke of control, we mentioned a moment in time *prior* to the manifestation in which a recognition of wanting/desiring something in that direction is required in order for the mind to feel in control. With inspiration, there is no such moment. Inspiration pops in of its own accord.

Yet, you do not sense the same ripples of loss of control as you would with a physical manifestation popping in of its own accord!

Inspiration is ever so slightly, ever so delicately, just outside the rules of the game.

Currently, that *feeling* of inspiration is so quickly molded into a *thought* that it is difficult for you to separate the two. Even your name for "inspiration" indicates the thing you are inspired to do or have. You do not have separate terms for the feeling of inspiration and the corresponding thought. Yet. You are, after all, still experiencing the 5 Senses BSC. You cannot stop, or undo, these mountains of beliefs. Nor would you want to, as so many others are still benefiting from them greatly.

Remember, when you are in pure flow there is nothing "to do." This is why we will not often give you processes, activities, or things to practice. Those would all be doing in a mind-based sense. That is practical for working within the confines of the 5 Senses BSC consciousness (and a powerful experience, too!).

Instead, we are having an enjoyable time of manifesting in a conscious way *what you are already expanding into*. It is that simple. And it is that potent.

Are you not beginning to see all that you already are?

You are imagining. Who cares if it's about acceptable things to the 5 Senses BSC? It is a miracle in this sea of limitation!

You are remembering. It does not matter if those memories nicely align to the 5 Senses BSC concept of a timeline, or even if you judge them to be good or bad.

You are feeling inspired. It is but a footnote to what that feeling of inspiration is about.

Beloved Ones, you are already transcending. And in this growing clarity you will find abundant freedom.

Momentum

Many others of the higher realms have reflected to you the idea of momentum – an ongoing energization of particular frequencies whose pull you can feel and, once aware of, may become a conscious belief that it is somehow harder to change.

This is the human conception of momentum. Let us share ours.

Momentum is the conscious embodiment of energization of a frequency. This 5 Senses reality you have built has momentum. Right now. Meaning, there are many who are resonating with the frequency and thus consciously embodying it.

You have momentum right now. You have eyes or ears that are part of a mind-body instrument perceiving these words.

Is it any harder to vibrate to a new frequency from this one, than it would be from any other frequency? Technically speaking, no.

Are you currently vibrating with a perception that believes it is difficult to break this cycle of limitation and experience anything else? Yes.

Momentum, as you see it, is your own beliefs – yet again – reinforcing the limitation, the lack, the difficulty, and the insufficiency. It is not a fundamental construct of energy in the universe.

You see the momentum in the bicycle careening downhill at a fast speed, which would be far more difficult to jump off of than at a slow speed. The momentum – your meaning – makes it difficult to change.

We see momentum as you energizing and embodying the experience of being out of control, which manifests in the experience of that bicycle. And, in a split second, you could just as easily embody a different frequency. This is just not yet a belief structure you have access to – it is not a frequency your consciousness has yet expanded to. That is all. The bicycle has no power over you! You are the creator of the experience of the bicycle.

You are extremely powerful.

All beings, all life, have a momentum. They *are* the conscious embodiment of whichever frequencies they are currently resonating. This is how we all experience creation. It is how *you* experience creation. *You* either become the conscious embodiment of a frequency, and by doing so demonstrate this frequency to others who perceive you. Or you perceive the conscious embodiment of another. You – and we all – *are life, are energy, are creation.*

If we were to take this concept more fluidly, we would say that right now you are building momentum in the New BSC while maintaining to a degree your momentum in the 5 Senses BSC. Both are expanding, active, and dynamic. As are you. Thus your oscillation between these embodiments has been just that – an oscillation. As was required in order to maintain the structure of this game.

Soon, though, the oscillation will turn to steady existence. Or said another way, the oscillation is accelerating to the point of being imperceptible. Thus, you will be more and more able to embody, to be present, to be *conscious of* the expansive New BSC.

And that is exactly what you have been doing here. Your consciousness is expanding into the parts of you that already have momentum in the New BSC.

The New BSC

Your consciousness is expanding. Resonance with those frequencies is manifesting a "new BSC" (to be named later). As you expand - consciously - you will have experiences of both, or each, BSC. You will oscillate.

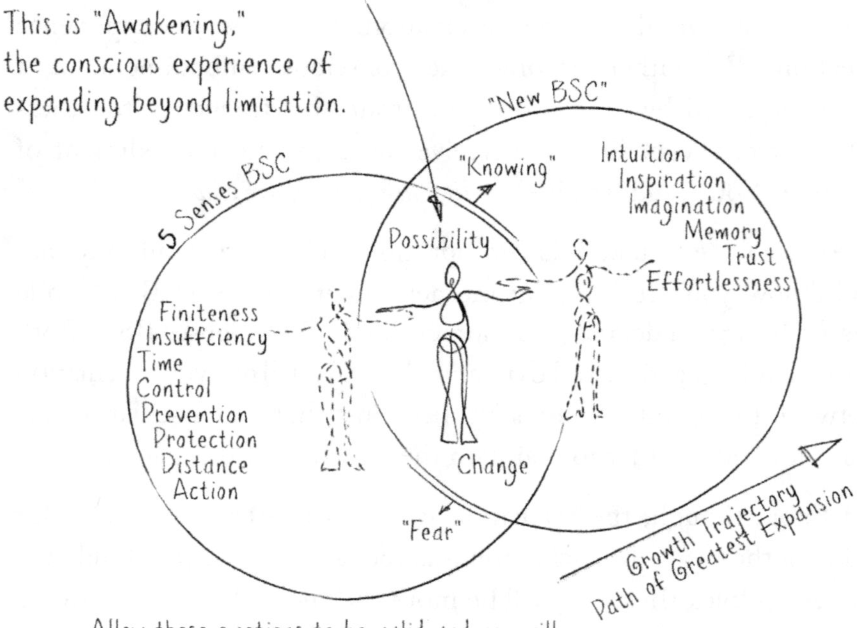

This is "Awakening," the conscious experience of expanding beyond limitation.

"New BSC"

"Knowing"

Intuition
Inspiration
Imagination
Memory
Trust
Effortlessness

5 Senses BSC

Possibility

Finiteness
Insuffciency
Time
Control
Prevention
Protection
Distance
Action

Change

"Fear"

Growth Trajectory
Path of Greatest Expansion

Allow these emotions to be valid and you will transcend them. Put another way, you will flow...

The beliefs of each BSC are valid, as the underlying frequencies of each BSC are perfect expressions of Creation.

Your preference for one over the other is your ability to navigate energy and detect your path of greatest expansion.

(Players from all layers or ribbons of your current 5 Senses BSC may join you in the "New BSC" should they so desire. See illustration 24).

Illustration 18: The New BSC

Chapter 9

Transcendence

Is it not wonderful to know that it is already underway? It is already happening? You have already achieved so much?

Many of you have been quite busy earning your awakening, we might say!

We have watched as new energy has gently found its way in – into new teachings, new ideas, new concepts of existence. And, oh, how amused we have been to watch you turn it into things you need "to do." You *try* to be more present. You exert great efforts to be allowing of your emotions. You think through all the pieces and what it will mean and how you will get to that transcended place. This is not your fault! This is no one's "fault." It is simply, beautifully, miraculously the very thorough way that the 5 Senses BSC can take even the most enlightened energies of pure radiant light and turn them into something that must be earned!

Beloved Ones, if you are reading this book, you already *are* in that transcended place. And into that space you will expand, expand, expand, and expand.

Effortlessness

We *love* this word. And you love this word too. Do you see, in that, we are already on similar wavelengths? You say, "But I do not have the ability to channel a book like this." Then it is simply not relevant to your path of greatest expansion. But, more importantly, you are already on these wavelengths with us! Receiving this information! Who cares who wrote it down?

Trust us. You have been here, in this perception of limitation, for billions of years. You have written things down many times!

We would suggest that your definition of effortlessness – as built, as allowed by the dynamic and vast, limiting energies of your BSC – does not even hold a candle to the true meaning of the term. But it is a start.

Energetically, as you experience it today, **effortlessness is the momentary cessation of your participation in the momentum of energies that dictate action in the 5 Senses BSC.** Said another way, for the briefest of moments you do not *believe* that anything could be required of you to make something happen. It is not wishing it could be easier. It is knowing that this is so.

This is in contrast to your conscious understanding of effortlessness. When you consciously desire something to be more effortless, you attempt to release your need to do all the things that had already been piling up on your to-do list that part of you *still believes needs to get done* by someone. In fact, this is often how you allow in your version of effortlessness – you ask somebody else to do it! It is very unusual for a human to desire effortlessness prior to that point of overwhelm.

Why is that?

Let us say you are planning a big event. A party, a celebration, a wedding, a surprise, a proposal, a presentation, a training, a speech, a trip … in all of these cases your mind has identified a moment at a future point in time by which the thing must take place or be accomplished.

It is the dreaded deadline.

Every time – and we mean *every time* – you place a marker on your future timeline, your belief systems will automatically, unconsciously and consciously, begin to work backward from that time and fill in the space with activities, actions, and efforts that will be required. Without your conscious knowing, you are actually working against the manifestation of the thing. For with each belief that gets built about what needs to be done, it makes it more and more difficult for that thing to manifest if those things *are not done*.

Can you call to mind that satisfying sensation of actually succeeding in checking all those boxes? This is right judgment by mind that, again, you call a sense of control. These things are related.

This is a perfect, impenetrable, masterpiece of limitation. For the more you plan, the more things arise that you must do. The more things arise that you must do, the more you are generating manifestation from a perspective of limitation ("must do") and building beliefs about the necessity of completing all of those things. The more those things manifest, the more you build beliefs about the lack of success of your planning and the more you build beliefs that *more* must be done to protect from and prevent such failures.

It is a marvel you ever achieve the things you "plan" to do!

Currently, your species is both surrounded by change (an aspect of the energy of the New BSC) and also planning, planning, planning further into the future than it has ever done (a balancing aspect of the 5 Senses BSC). Your governments, your scientific organizations, your space programs – all are planning decades and even centuries into the future. (Careful though, do not blame *them*! You are all participating in the construction of the playing field after all!) And the list of things that must be done grows and grows. And then you all are very busy and very tired. And time "flies by."

You now could see that for someone to desire effortlessness in the midst of this is important indeed. To feel, to sense, to connect to a concept that is an alternate path, is a vital, living, and breathing reflection of the New BSC.

If you would like to go in the direction of the 5 Senses BSC, you can plan, work, toil, revise, earn, protect from, and prevent. You can try to map out all the things you will need to do over the coming days, weeks, months, or years. And your mind will be very busy indeed. A delicious, limiting experience you can really sink your teeth into.

If you would like to go in the direction of the New BSC, you imagine, remember, and feel inspired (notice we did not say "follow" your inspiration – you are not obligated to *do* anything with that inspiration!). You will become more aware of all the ideas that feel even slightly more effortless.

And your mind will say, "At long last! I and consciousness are not hooked together. I can manage the incoming sensations from the 5 senses, and consciousness will stretch its wings outward to the perception of even more energies. I will be aware, awakened, and transcendent." Mind gets a vacation. Mind is no longer constantly activating all sorts of beliefs and judgments in order to "keep" you alive (notice: another all-important limiting area of your belief system – unless you *do* things to keep yourselves alive, you will inevitably perish). Mind gets to drive the car on autopilot – beautifully, perfectly, and easily – while the new capacities of your expanded consciousness select new and different frequencies far, far further up the chain of manifestation than thought was ever able to go.

Attention

This is not an uncomplicated conversation for us to have! For we are discussing – on a mind-based, 5 senses level – the actual limitations of your mind and all the things that it cannot sense but that "you" (your consciousness) will one day sense.

Do you see the paradox? And we did it all by playing by the rules of time! If we had hands, or arms, we would pat ourselves on the back! We tease!

But this is required because currently your consciousness, the "you" from this vantage point, is aligned to the limitations of the 5 Senses BSC "mind." Thus we must… we are… we can speak to *both*.

And we would suggest – powerfully so – that you are already experiencing this difference.

Particularly as children, you often hear the command: "Focus!" How many toddlers, children, and even teens have been told numerous times to focus – on putting on their coats, on their schoolwork, on the activity their bodies should be doing but their minds are not?

Now, before we activate the giant swaths of belief systems about guilt – for you all have a great deal of guilt where your young are concerned – let us discuss why this is.

You are assisting these young in integrating into the fabric of the game. It is a required, perfect process of this BSC.

As we mentioned before, you are constantly being birthed into this Belief System Complex (BSC). The human aging process, from our perspective, is a series of increasingly limited experiences here in the game. Someone who is 30 years old is not as deeply enmeshed in the beliefs of limitation as someone who is 80 years old. This is why you often look at each other, across ages, and wonder, "How can they think that?" You attribute it, of course, to time, to being of different eras. In truth, you are not yet connected to the beliefs that they are. You have not yet reached that point.

Some among you believe that your children are done growing sometime around their late teens or early twenties, and then they are "adults." This is not so. With each day, with each year, their belief systems will evolve. You are each as much children as you are adults in every moment of your existence here. Keep this in mind as you look at your toddler – she is exactly like you, just in a different corner of the experience of this BSC.

This may feel oppressive or inescapable. Keep in mind that this is because your perspective from the 5 Senses BSC is activated. *It is built to believe this about the aging process.* If you did *not* feel like aging was oppressive or inescapable, it wouldn't quite be your experience of aging!

If you felt like aging was not oppressive, you might choose it more joyfully, which would change the nature of the aging process (for joy is more allowing than resistance). And if you felt like aging was not inescapable, you might choose something else! Which means you couldn't experience the feeling of something being inescapable!

Love these feelings of disallowance. They represent the loyal and powerful way this BSC has helped you to experience some of the most unique frequencies in all of creation.

DETERIORATION

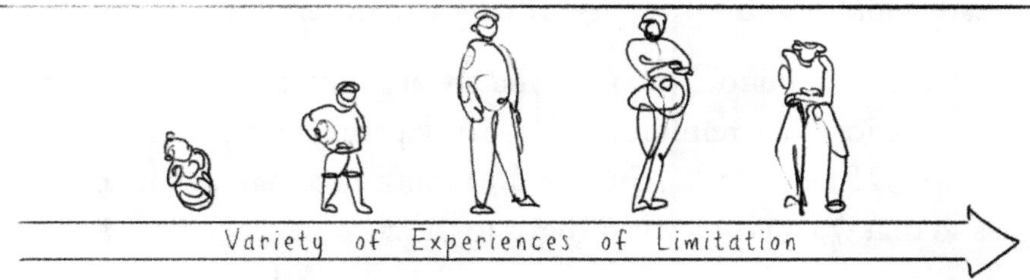

You are always being "birthed" into this "reality," into this BSC.

From the moment of conception, your deepening connection to the vast matrices grows.

You experience lack and limitation in varied ways until your participation is complete.

All have - historically - obeyed the core values, core frequency, of the BSC because changes would alter the perfect playground of limitation you had consructed. And many wanted to participate.

But now, many of you have a desire for change.

You are capable of imagining more.
You are capable of wishing for more.
You have thoughts about how it could be "better."

Thus, the manifestations of a change in the frequency of the BSC you participate in have already begun.

You do not un-do the BSC you are coming from. You build a new one.

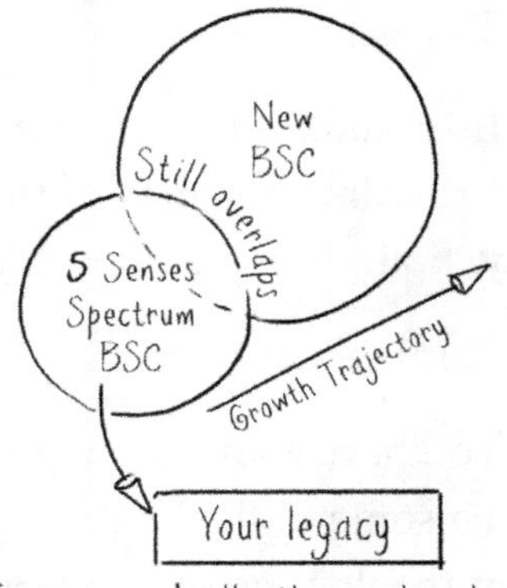

For any and all others who should ever benefit by participating on their paths of greatest expansion.

You do not yet understand what an amazing gift of contrast you have given to the galaxies.
But others do.
And, one day, you will too.

Illustration 19: Deterioration

And also know that, if you can perceive these words, you are already vibrating toward a new BSC and a different experience.

When you are told to focus, you are actually receiving a powerful manifestation that reinforces your participation in belief systems of limitation. Energetically, **focus is the rebuffing or narrowing of energies so that what is perceived aligns to the current capacities of mind.**

Let us explain.

When you are watching your favorite television show, and it is at a particularly intense moment of action, how aware are you of everything else going on in your room? In your house? On your street? When your mother or partner stomps into the room a moment later and angrily says, "I've been calling you for five minutes!" are you surprised that you did not hear him or her?

This is focus.

In dramatic film moments when someone is defusing a bomb or staring into the eyes of their true love, the rest of the world fades away. Sounds, smells, and sights beyond these points are muted.

This is focus.

You have a joke among your kind that when an elderly person is having some difficulty driving and the radio is on, they shout, "Turn down the volume so I can see!"

This is focus: a stripping out, a narrowing, a rebuffing of the perception of 5 Senses stimuli in order to align to a narrowed capacity of mind.

How interesting, is it not, that when you are learning something new, you often feel compelled to "focus." When you are finding a concept difficult to grasp, you go somewhere quiet. When you are trying to listen to someone's complicated speech, you close your eyes.

You know this quite well. You have even studied the squishy substrate you call your brain to understand how it creates maps and frameworks in order to constantly strip out stimuli and make decisions more rapidly. You have become aware that there is a great deal of your day-to-day lives that you do not "see."

It is the constant, dynamic action of the limiting BSC made manifest.

What then, is attention? How does this differ from focus?

From our vantage point, they are very critically, very powerfully different. For one expands to the furthest point possible currently for consciousness, the other is the furthest extent of what you call "mind" – and that we call the limitations of the 5 Senses BSC.

Energetically, **attention is the expansion of your perception of energies to the furthest point possible.** At the present moment in your timeline, this supersedes, *just slightly* but all-importantly, the current limitations of the mind.

Let us return to the example of driving the car. When you are focused on driving, you are often staring at the lanes in front of you, taking into account the key markers your mental frameworks have identified for "safe" driving.

Let us say that you hear a loud crash to the side of you, and a passenger simultaneously shouts, "Pay attention!" Does your field of perception narrow or expand? Do you strip everything out to stare at just the bumper in front of you, or do you expand as quickly as possible to take in as much as you can?

Correct, perception expands.

You jerk your head up, engage your peripheral vision, glance at your mirrors, grip the steering wheel more tightly, prepare to move your foot rapidly, etc.

You expand – ever so slightly – outward. As far as your senses and your choices of action will allow you to do.

Beloved, the fact that we could give you this example, the way the differences between these two things resonate within you, is but a first and miraculous step toward the New Belief System Complex (nBSC).

To be focused is to double down on the limitations of the 5 Senses BSC manifested concept of the "mind."

To be attentive is to receive, through all possible levels of your being, all energies of which you may be conscious.

Have you ever noticed that if you are "paying attention," you notice slight and subtle things about the room or a dear friend? Without your analysis, you make a remark based on that observation, and it leads to a very important connection with that dear friend that uplifts you both. Had you been focused on what you needed to talk about, or focused on your mental to-do list, or on judging yourself as you walked up to that friend – might you have missed that subtle observation?

This difference between focus and attention is no less colossal than, no less important than, the differences between two Belief System Complexes.

And you will find, *effortlessly*, that you are more often drawn to paying attention than to focusing.

SUBCONSCIOUS

CONSCIOUS: simply, another name for 5 Senses manifestation.

The limits of mind's attention.

The current extent of mental capacity.

The ability to name, via thought or words a specific thing, belief, emotion, habit, idea...

SUBCONSCIOUS: simply, the identification of mind's limits and things occuring "beyond" mind.

(Subconscious is not lurking around or beneath you. It is all within you and beyond...)

The distance between Conscious and Subconscious is the shift from when you are "unaware" of something to when you are aware of it. Your capacity to be "aware" is your moving beyond the (narrowing) focus on mind's bandwidths/wavelengths.

FOCUS

= a narrowing of energies. Putting limits on which or how many energies may be percived at one "time." A stripping out, rebuffing, narrowing to fit mind's capacity.

"Shh!
Be quiet!
I have to
focus!"

Presence in belief system activation

ATTENTION

=the ability to apply your existence to a variety of wavelengths. Receptive of ALL frequencies you as an entity are able to receive.

Attentive mind = Receptive mind

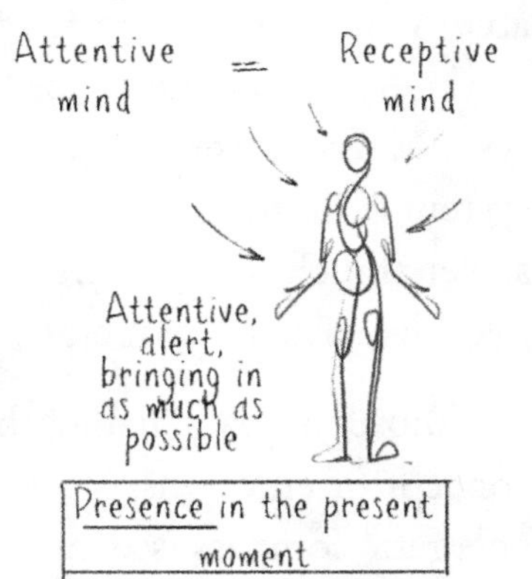
Attentive,
alert,
bringing in
as much as
possible

Presence in the present moment

Illustration 20: Subconscious

Trust

There is more evidence that you are already transcending, Beloved. And your ability to bring this to consciousness so easily is but more and growing reflections of your expansion to broader frequencies.

How interesting, how wonderful, how powerful to have this experience. To still be partially limited by the 5 Senses BSC so that you can have the experience of awakening to this knowledge. Of reading a book that tells you these things. So that you can feel, with that beautiful part of yourself – the emotions – all the tantalizing energies of contrast between limitation and pure flow. What an incredible experience indeed.

Though the flavor, the version, the way in which you experience your emotions are influenced, of course, by the frequency with which you are currently resonating, your emotions are *yours*. They are a part of you. A unique part of you. This is nothing less than your infinite ability to discern between and to choose energetic frequencies. It is a core part of your being. Though you may be able to manifest them in different ways – technically, in infinite ways – you can never be without your own energetic guidance system. Even here. Even from the depths of this colossal belief system of limitation, where you cut yourselves off from perceiving so very much, *still* you are able to discern between energies. This has manifested as human emotion.

Those of us outside the egg adore, revel in, celebrate your concept of emotions. To see such a unique reflection of your own energetic compass is an amazing fascination! We will never, ever tire of hearing humans laugh!

You all think, in your current conception of life forms, that other beings "out there" must have emotions too. They must also war, they must also battle, they must also feel revenge and sacrifice. They must also triumph, they must also be peaceful, they must also feel generous.

Beloved, you are still awakening to the uniqueness that is you, all the way down to what has manifested on these wavelengths. Though you have given yourself the experience of perceiving so little, remember that, even here, the fundamental uniqueness of all life cannot be denied.

Humanity is very, very special.

Can you trust this knowing that is inside of you?

And what is *trust* exactly?

Earlier we described that there is a point of pure light, in the midst of all this disallowing, at which your participation in this BSC is momentarily released. You call this point "love." It is but a beginning, a jumping off point into a sea of infinite wavelengths of pure flow.

Just beside that point of love, is a frequency that you call "trust."

When you trust something, your physical and mental form relaxes. This you are aware of; this you know. There is a release, a letting go, a handing over of all those judgments, worries, and things to do and to be accomplished to the thing you are trusting – be it a process, a friend, a machine, or a deity. Energetically, **trust is the momentary cessation in the participation of the energies (and beliefs) associated with time.** Thus, not as complete of a release of the BSC as is love, but a major release of the fundamental underpinning of this experience.

In your release of time, a great number of beliefs soften. You are not as worried, as agitated, because you are no longer activating all the judgments about "when" and "how." ("How" being a version of "when" that is constructed by action, which is heavily based on the passage of time. You see "when" and "how" as different, but in actuality, they are both versions of time-based assessments of energy expenditure. Without time, the many questions and plans you make in order to address "how" would greatly soften.)

We have a question: why does your kind currently watch so much television and film?

You would likely say something to the effect of your brains being addicted to it.

All right. But then, *energetically*, why is your brain addicted to it? What does it represent?

This may sound strange to you, but watching television is a version of trust.

Let us visit these moments in detail.

You come home from a long day of daily life in the 5 Senses BSC. You get all the evening things done that you "need" to and have a small window of time (time!) left before you must re-energize your physical form with sleep. You crave a "break," a "reality escape" from all that pesky action of the mind that has been so active, so persistent all day. You are drawn to the idea of watching a show. Any kind of show.

You sit down on the couch, you grab the remote, you turn on the television, and what happens? The action of your belief systems softens. There is nothing you need to worry about, right now. There is nothing you need to do, right now. For this brief window of time, the only action that "needs" to take place is for you to watch this show. Everything else can be released. And all your belief systems say, "Well, alright."

Now, what do the majority of your shows and films contain? Great, dramatic explorations of frequencies of disallowing! So you do not exactly escape your BSC, do you? And then what happens after the show? You activate great belief systems about action and time, and time wasted watching that show! We can't help you there. You are still part of this game, after all. We tease.

Yet still, for those windows of time, what you are very softly, very delicately exploring is the energetic frequency of trust.

Let us look at another version of this in your present-day societies.

What is your technology, energetically? What is this era that has been characterized by machines that do things for humans? It is a version of trust, which is the gradual or momentary cessation of participation in beliefs about time.

Is life not just a little more effortless than it was 500 years ago? Do you not have machines that wash clothes, machines that transport you, machines that connect you to people far away? Is it not a beautiful manifestation of the gentle release of the concept of time? Things get done more quickly, you travel more quickly, you speak to others more quickly. Time in the context of technology is very flexible indeed. It should be no surprise that you can already *imagine* ways in which technology could potentially circumvent time all together. It is because you are all trusting more – that is, you are releasing, gradually and gently, your beliefs about time.

We understand. You may say, "But there are still moments when I don't completely *trust* the machines." Of course. That is a moment of disallowance in your experience of the manifestation, and that is quite possible from the 5 Senses BSC vantage point. Yet, the trend, the aggregate, the momentum of these developments is a reflection of growing trust – that is, release of beliefs about time.

Here we should also note that when humans look to a person, institution, or belief system in which to place their trust, this is a conscious experience of releasing these beliefs. Though at different places on the scale, can you see how releasing something in prayer to a deity you trust is akin to the feeling, to the sensations, of letting it all go and curling up on the couch with a device? Kin in emotion, they are! Though you do have great, monstrous mountains of belief about the differences between these two things.

"But," you say, "there is so little trust in our societies! I don't trust anyone of *that* political faction/religion/administration/group!"

Who says you have to?

Please understand, Beloved, that the friction you are all feeling right now about all of these groups who are not believing what you believe comes from a desire in and of itself. *You desire to exist in a world, in a place, where you can trust others.* You desire to exist *in trust*, which means, outside the binding actions of time.

When you see evidence of beliefs, of actions, that you do not trust – that is, which you judge as being something you must protect from and prevent – you activate great swaths of disallowance. *The friction you feel is this friction between your desire to trust others and the judgment of 5 senses stimuli that tells you that you cannot or should not.*

You may soften this in one of two ways. You can release your judgments and beliefs about prevention and protection (you are already doing this as you expand into the New BSC). You may also soften your need to trust others. You may choose, in any moment, to trust your connection and yourself.

Let us back up the chain a little bit to that desire for trusting others, for this is important.

Before that desire turned into a thought, "I want to trust others," it was pure energy. And that energy reflects newness, flow, and expansive frequencies. It is molded, molded, molded into one of the most expansive things possible on this frequency, which is currently trust (which vibrates closely to love). And without your conscious say-so, the beliefs of your BSC are activated and mold this further into the very, very specific concept of "I want to trust *others.*"

This first thought is a manifestation, and manifestation is energy that has been filtered and molded by way of the BSC.

Your mind, which is the conscious embodiment of the frequency of limitation, takes in all manifestations on the 5 Senses wavelengths and evaluates whether or not this manifestation – something to trust – has occurred, is evidenced.

When it judges the stimuli to be not-yet-trustworthy, you feel a particular kind of conscious friction that you call danger, risk, betrayal, or, more softly, disappointment.

Unconsciously, massive portions of the BSC are activated to deny, to fight against, to avoid this sense of friction. And beliefs are instantly built about how to do away with this friction, namely prevention and protection, which lead to ideas of conflict with the source of betrayal and disappointment, namely, your opposing faction. And as is with the great cycle of limitation here, it energizes itself perpetually.

We have just outlined the underlying, energetic constructs of your "war."

Whether it be at the level of a disagreement between two individuals or two countries.

The threat feels present and real to you because the friction is so great. Only here, Beloved, could anything be *un*-trustworthy. Only here could something ever disappoint you. Only here could you ever be *not* in control. You have had to create much, energize much, to give yourselves an experience that is so opposite to everything outside the egg. And *the more you expand*, the more strongly you will feel these energies outside the egg, and the more acutely you will become aware of this friction.

This is what is happening in your societies today.

You are, simply, awakening.

We know. We hear your question already as this calls to mind the manifestations of war, strife, and loss: "But what do we *do*?"

Remember, mind-based action is the collision of desire and the recognition that what is desired is not "here" yet. So let us assist you in recognizing that it is here already.

There is already a person whom you can trust infinitely, and that is yourself. This is not about manifestation! This is not about how you "should" trust what you do, say, look like, choose, create, or any other manifested demonstration of body and mind. You will continue to judge these things for a little while longer, as you still have one foot in the 5 Senses BSC. Do not run from these judgments of self. Love them, and you will transcend them. Love everything this BSC has given you the opportunity to experience.

But also, notice something more ...

Do you imagine?

Do you remember?

From time to time, do you feel inspired?

Do you feel more attentive to your life, to your existence here? (Let us answer this one for you: yes! Or you would not be reading these words!)

Do you have moments of trust in others as well as yourself?

Do you watch television sometimes? Or use machines to do things for you?

Does love feel lighter to you than hate?

Does trust feel nicer than panic?

TRUST

One of the greatest limiting beliefs you created is your inability to TRUST without physical manifestation.

Since energy precedes manifestation, your need (beliefs) to first see manifestation hinders the flow greatly!

You did not trust your own feelings – that is, your energetic peceptions of light.

↳ This lack of trust grew. You perceived, acknowledged, consciously heeded, less and less of what you felt.

↳ Beliefs about needing manifestation GREW. By these beliefs you were increasingly surprised, fooled, disappointed, disheartened.

So integral are these beliefs to your BSC, you are not consciously aware of many at all.

You do not wonder at all how this could be possible in an infinite universe, where your own perception of the energy of all is also infinite?

- That things can be hidden by paper, metal, or distance?
- That you could be lied to or led astray?
- That the choices, actions, or beliefs of another could ever surprise you?
- That someone could sneak up behind you and scare you!?

You have created obscurity, shadow, opacity, disguise, deceit... By believing you must first see the evidence in your 5 Senses Spectrum, you built a vast machine of blindness, of ignorance, to all the perception and knowing that comes through to you on energetic wavelengths.

Creating the perfect playing field of abundant limitation.

And now, You are expanding beyond this.

Illustration 21: Trust

Do you see how you are already guiding yourselves home?

Gently, Beloved. Lovingly, Beloved. You are all and everything you ever dreamed you would be. Everything you hoped to achieve here has been achieved. You radiate an abundant light to all others through this most glorious experience of contrast. It is beautiful.

We see you. We have seen you all along. You have never been deficient. You have never needed to earn. You have never needed to change, to stop, to prevent anything in this vast creation.

But by your beliefs, you have built something extraordinary, which will benefit the galaxies for untold millennia to come.

Part 3

What You Are About to Experience

So much, Beloved Ones! So much you have learned and absorbed so far! We would like to point out to you that knowledge is a frequency, and this is but a manifestation of it. This could manifest in infinite ways. What matters most is the frequency. Your mind may "space out" or come and go here and there as you read, and that is of no matter. The connection to this frequency is yours, is absorbed, becomes a part of you. The manifested thoughts that reflect this frequency will appear for you when the time is right. Perfectly.

Even so, let us review where we have been so far for the benefit of mind:

Currently your **energetic perception** is limited to the frequencies detected by what you call the **5 Senses,** which we loosely describe as the **frequencies of current resonance** (touch, taste, and smell) and the **frequencies of imminent resonance** (sound and sight).

The **mind** is your concept for what must orchestrate the collaboration between body and senses. In actuality, your beliefs are the orchestrating "brain," to which you are deeply connected. Additionally, your conscious awareness is currently limited to the capacity of mind, which at this time is just ever-so-slightly beyond the limits of the 5 Senses.

Until recent times, mind-based action, or **choices,** were unconsciously directed by the dynamic action of the Belief System Complex (BSC).

This dynamic action is perpetually reinforcing or **cyclical.** Beliefs affect manifestation and the perception of it, and manifestation builds beliefs. This cycle continually escalates – or rebalances – the limitation against the incoming, pure energy of flow, to which you are infinitely connected by virtue of the structure of creation and your existence.

As part of your **awakening** – the conscious expansion from the frequencies of limitation – several loopholes have been introduced into the cycle and are being used by your kind to build what we may now call a **New Belief System Complex (nBSC).**

Most notably, the concept of **change,** which allows for things that were once not possible to be possible. The 5 Senses BSC balances, that is, remains intact, around this loophole via the concept of **control.**

Additionally, **inspiration,** much like memory and imagination, is a loophole that allows in new energy in a way that does not disrupt the accepted tenets of finiteness and insufficiency. This is balanced by the 5 Senses BSC through the concept of **action,** or required expenditures of energy in order to make unmanifested ideas manifest, thus energizing the lack of manifestation.

Momentum – or the conscious embodiment of a given frequency – is the driving force behind the awakening, as each member of creation may and does choose with which frequency to resonate. You are as of yet unconscious of your choice – as was desired in order to experience awakening – but will be soon.

An indication of this expanded conscious perception is the growing difference between the sensations of **focus** (a narrowing of 5 senses stimuli) and **attention** (the conscious perception of energies from all possible levels of being).

As beliefs about required mind-body action are softening, experiences of **effortlessness** are increasing. As beliefs about time are softening, experiences of **trust** are increasing (the oft-said, "It *will* work out").

War and conflict are manifestations of the energetic friction between the new energies you are perceiving by way of your awakening, and the dynamic action of the 5 Senses BSC that evaluates manifested stimuli for evidence of this immense sense of trust and finds none. The gap, the distance, between these two things feels like danger, risk, betrayal, and disappointment. These emotions – which are perceptions of disallowance – are deeply connected to vast portions of beliefs that instigate intensely felt actions of prevention and protection. You do not go to war lightly, do you?

Would it surprise you to know that, epochs ago, you did?

You do not go lightly today because the limitations, the beliefs, are deeper and more acute. Your action and movement in this reality are all so constricted, as is part of the experience you desired. And these things *feel* so heavy to you because you are becoming conscious of your preference for something else – for lightness, for trust, for love.

But at one point, you preferred things other than light, love, and trust. You preferred the limitation. And it did not feel the way it does today. You spent glorious epochs in energized limitation! You will remember this, in your own way, in your own time, for remembering is an important step on the path of your transcendence.

Chapter 10

Lifetimes

Let us begin by exploring your concept of "a life" within the context of the beliefs of time, and then without. And from there we can continue to build on that clarity.

Your beliefs about time unconsciously construct a "reality" – that is, what you perceive on the spectra of the 5 Senses – in which you are only capable of perceiving the "present time."

If a human, from their mind-based perspective, were to define a time period, they would often rely on the structure of events, of manifestations, to do this. They would look to action and things that "took place" to define a period of time. In so doing, they reinforce, they energize, the idea that action and events are *the* defining characteristics of time and of "reality." Thus, the beliefs in time are reinforced, meaning that if you cannot perceive the actions and events of another time on the 5 Senses Spectrum, you are in fact incapable of perceiving that time.

No sight, sound, touch, taste, or smell of that time period could be perceived, and thus you are *not in* that time period. If your 5 Senses perceive this time period, then you *are in* this time period. The limited perceptions of mind are satisfied. You know where you are. You even have a squeak and a whistle to match – you give the time a name, i.e., the day, month, and year. (Here we highlight how entangled are the concepts of time and distance. Keep in mind, Beloved, that these beliefs are fluid and dynamic, though we delineate here for the purposes of clarity).

This is the conscious definition of time. Now let us take a step outward and look at these concepts of time from a slightly broader energetic vantage point. Almost all of which has been unconscious to you until now, as that is the way you wanted it.

The idea of a time period has a vast number of energetic characteristics attached to it: what is possible, what is not, what has already been done, what has not, etc. Essentially, *all the current agreements of the BSC* are the defining elements of what you call a "time period." Pretty amazing, is it not? You take all those vast, colossal mountains and oceans of beliefs and agreements, and mold and filter the energy through them, and out it all pops into a very, very specific squeak and whistle that is the day, month, and year.

Incredible!

And, moreover, *you all agree* to this molded energy so that day, month, and year *mean exactly the same thing to each of you.*

"One moment, please," you might say. "Though we all may say we are in the year 3000, my *experience* of that year could be really different than my friend's. Some people have good years, and some people have terrible years, right?"

If you are talking in terms of what was received on the 5 Senses Spectrum, then you are correct. It is unlikely that both you and your friend manifested the *exact same series of manifestations* within that year. Uniqueness is reflected, even here! However, the underlying, unconscious constructs, through which that energy was molded before it became your manifestations and your friend's manifestations, were the same.

Dimensions

Until now, we have avoided as much as possible using the words "physical" and "dimension," as you have already built a great deal of beliefs about these squeaks and whistles. And yet, they are the best proxies for what this energy will convey, and so we will proceed.

Recall that by our definition, "reality" is quite simply how you perceive energetic frequencies. Currently, consciously, your perception of energy is by way of the 5 Senses. This is what you define as real and reality.

We perceive energetic frequencies in quite a few more ways than that. Thus our "reality," what we consider to be real, is different.

As you expand in what you are able to perceive, what you consider "real" will also expand.

If in 1,000 years your mind-body instrument has evolved to perceive infrared spectra via your eyesight, you would be able to "see" more things than you can today. However, if you stood next to someone from this time period, when you would say, "I see someone on the infrared spectrum walking through the room," your companion of this time period would reply, "I don't see it. Prove it. I don't think what you're seeing is real." And by the definition of reality, for them, they would be completely accurate. They don't perceive that energy, but you do.

Using your beliefs in space and distance, you might say that energy, that possibility, is "in" your reality but not theirs. From a certain vantage point, this is accurate. However, from another vantage point, an equally valid perspective would be that technically the energy is everywhere. Both of you receive the light of all creation by being creation, you just molded it differently into different experiences – one where you can see infrared, and one where you cannot. Said another way, it is you that have the potential to be everywhere, not realities.

By this definition, there could be as many different realities as there are beings in creation. Correct! Absolutely, beautifully, fantastically correct!

And we would suggest, Beloved One, that it is equally possible and valid to hold a belief that diversity of realities is healthy and beneficial as it is to say that diversity of realities is dangerous and precipitates chaos (the latter being more akin to present-day beliefs about dimensions in the 5 Senses BSC). They are each beliefs – and a **belief is a way of molding energy into experience.** And by way of experience, you expand more fully into yourself and all that you are. *Thus, there is not a single belief, in all of creation, that is invalid.* And there is not a single belief, in all of creation, that is "better," as you would say, than any other belief.

Beliefs are just a way of creating with energy to experience energy. And there are – blessedly, beautifully, miraculously – infinite ways to create.

We have established that you live in a consensus-driven reality. By way of participation in this BSC, you all abide by a similar set of rules, which trickle down into what you perceive on the 5 Senses Spectrum.

Are all realities consensus-driven? No.

So it would be possible to have a reality of one? Yes. Where only that one, in all of creation, perceives energy in that particular way.

Would it be possible to have one reality of billions? Yes, and indeed, that is what you are experiencing here. Billions of you agree to perceive energy in a vastly similar way, and to reinforce that reality by your participation in it.

Would it be possible to have one reality for zillions, for maybe even more than for which we have squeaks and whistles? Now *that* is an interesting question.

But first we have a question for you: is a Belief System Complex (BSC) the same thing as a "dimension"?

Let us begin by reviewing, generally, the beliefs you have already built about this squeak. (Because a squeak is a manifestation, and manifestations build beliefs in your fantastic, cyclical, limiting complex!)

A dimension, by current perspective, is a "place" different than the time and space in which you currently exist, mentally and physically. Sometimes you think there are three of them or five of them or eleven of them, sometimes you think there might be many more. Sometimes you believe you are "in" the third dimension and moving toward a different one. Sometimes you think alternate dimensions are just like your current dimension, except for a few key differences. Perhaps the outcome of a war was different in that other dimension, or humanity learned and does different things – thereby defining dimension by differences in action as perceived by the 5 Senses (which is in some ways similar to how you define a time period by the 5 Senses, is it not?). Sometimes you think there may be as many different dimensions as there are earths, or galaxies, thereby defining dimension by points in time and space.

The idea of "different dimensions" can and has caused a little bit of discomfort as well. How would you navigate "back" to your dimension if you visit another one? Do you choose to go to one, or could you fall into it accidentally? Oh, our Beloved Ones, how do you keep coming up with this stuff? Yet another belief about being not-in-control, set to balance the limitation against some most expansive thinking. Our greatest appreciation to you and what you build!

And no, a dimension cannot jump out and get you! Oh, how we laugh! We love you so much!

We will explain.

If currently, your idea of dimension is generally based upon definitions of action, time, and place (or space, as you say), then the concepts of "dimension" and "reality" are heavily overlapping, are they not? All these things you use to describe a possible alternate dimension are really different ways in which you perceive energy via the 5 Senses – places, distance, body, action, etc. This is your current reality, we would agree, but dimension is slightly different from our vantage point.

We consider a **dimension to be the experience of a composite of wavelengths.**

Recall that we described your current experience of limitation as one that might be described as a staccato, or a singularity, in which you are predominantly unaware of the frequencies just beside you. Moreover, if a being does not completely align to the wavelength with which you are resonating (perhaps they are broader or vaster), you are unable to perceive said being. Thus, your experience of creation is vastly limited. You are completely unaware of all that you are surrounded by.

We can understand how, from your vantage point and the limitations of your current consciousness, you might well be able to perceive the concept of a dimension, but the limiting action of your Belief System Complex (BSC) would diminish this concept into being a possible replica of staccatos, or singularities, somewhere "out there" that are possible to experience. Other dimensions being of slightly different action, time, or place.

In actuality, dimensions are composites of wavelengths that are experienced by beings, often collectively.

To this point, we have been focused on the concept of your Belief System Complex (BSC) and how that functions in your experience of energy and existence.

Let us zoom out from that concept just slightly.

Imagine, for a moment, that your 5 Senses BSC is a beautiful bubble of dynamic light floating in the vast ocean of the infinite universe. Such a beautiful, buoyant bubble! You have been having *such* an amazing experience inside this BSC. In fact, a great many have been enjoying this BSC!

And, also, you might notice a little bubble growing and expanding from this BSC. This is the New BSC (nBSC) that you are building, of which we have spoken. Heavily overlapping for now, but one day the connection between these two may be released.

Now, stand atop these two conjoined, beautiful bubbles of light and look around you. Peer out into the infinite space out there.

Is it empty?

Is it a vast nothingness beyond your bubbles?

Do you see an endless void?

Are you alone?

Our most Beloved, our most cherished, our most adored ones – we are filled with so much love when we tell you that no, you are not!

You are surrounded by such beautiful wavelengths of love and light and *life* in *all directions*! Such beings, such existences, such experiences as you have never known nor – from within your BSC – could have imagined! Ways of being, ways of manifesting, in such diversity, float around you on the most beautiful wavelengths of infinite light!

And now you see that. Now you look down and realize how much your BSC has been a point of light, vibrating on a very narrow, very specific frequency. How glorious! How uncannily specific! And now you look around you and see more bubbles – of all different kinds and shapes and sizes and varieties of light. Moving and floating about you, above you, below you, around you. And you realize that some, many in fact, span more broadly than your BSC. In fact, so many of them reach across all sorts of wavelengths of light.

They are all fluid. Sometimes they pass each other without touching. Sometimes they brush each other very delicately. Sometimes several of them come together in radiant light and conjoin and span even more frequencies. Sometimes they move apart.

And now you look down and realize that from within the 5 Senses BSC radiates one single thread of delicate light. That thread moves in a straight line outward, through the New BSC, and beyond it, out into this space, so full and abundant with bubbles of light and wavelengths of beauty. And that delicate thread very gently, very lovingly, connects to quite a few other bubbles of light.

This thread is the Bridge of Light that has been built for you. To emerge, should you wish, from the 5 Senses BSC. And by that emergence, contribute to the building of the New BSC (nBSC), and from such a vantage point, choose any next experience you wish.

And we, Beloved, are the bubbles that gently connect to this emerging thread.

Hierarchy

It is all right, Beloved, if mind "freaks out" a little bit, as you would say, at this imagery, at this analogy. For as we have described, currently what you call your mind is actually the dynamic, orchestrating actions of your belief systems. And in this example, you have moved very clearly outside the bounds of those beliefs. In response, the belief systems balance the limitation by asking seemingly critical questions, "What does this all mean? How would we navigate all of this? How did we not know this was happening? Is this safe?"

Remember, Beloved, love these thoughts and the related emotions – perceptions – of disallowance. They represent the experience of limitation that was so very perfect, indeed. We can answer all of these questions, and we will. For that is part of how you walk the bridge, so to speak, it is part of how you move into more expansive beliefs, which are these more expansive frequencies.

What does this all mean? It means you are awakening. That is, moving through a conscious experience of expanding to broader frequencies. Realizing that there are such broader frequencies is an important first step!

How can you navigate all of this? By way of your infinite, unbreakable, infallible ability to perceive the differences in energy. Which, even here, has been intact. Your name for this guidance system from within the 5 Senses BSC is emotion. As you move toward broader frequencies, this capacity to read the differences in energy will also naturally expand, while also becoming more conscious.

How did you not know this was happening? By choice. It is difficult to have a conscious experience of limited experience if you are simultaneously aware of all the things you were supposed to be limited from being conscious of!

Is this safe? Beloved, you must create the experience of not being safe. Thus, this is your belief in things not being safe activating itself. That is all. Can you choose to continue to create not-being-safe? Yes. Can you choose to allow in infinite safety? Yes. That choice is yours. We will not make it for you. (And how will you make that choice? See the answers above!)

Let us return to our bubbles and talk about these concepts a little further.

Would you consider each of these bubbles to be a "dimension" or another fluid, evolving, dynamic Belief System Complex (BSC)?

We would like to share with you our vantage point.

But first, it would be helpful if we spoke a little bit about who we are, which we have not done yet.

The "voice" you hear in this work is actually the result of a collection of beings from different bubbles, energetically combining their perspectives (down to these very specific words – not bad, we would say!). This is why it can feel so enlightening. It is not a singular new belief coming into manifestation – which can also feel enlightening, in its way. This book represents the conscious perception of energy from a composite of wavelengths.

By virtue of the design of your bubble, of your egg, of your Belief System Complex (BSC), we had been unable to connect to all that you are. Energetically, of course, there were still parts of you that we could perceive – that part of you that was resonating on this very specific frequency. But beyond that, we knew naught. For it was by design that you should be cut off, imperceptible of broader frequencies, which is where we resonate.

Said another way, our consciousness could not expand to your wavelengths and be perceptible by you, unless we, too, narrowed our consciousness to the specific frequency of your game. Thus, we knew you were having the time of your lives within the BSC, but we were unable to join, to connect, to learn from your experiences. (And we will be honest, we've been having the time of our lives in our own frequencies, revelrous in this experience of seeming disconnection with you!)

This was the perfect, expansive setup, until it was time for one among you to build the bridge of light.

She built it from deep within your Belief System Complex (BSC), from the depths of limitation. In fact, she has undergone limitation some of you will never need to experience. But she did. For, in order to build a bridge of light to which *all* could connect, from anywhere within your *vast* BSC, she needed to experience *all possible frequencies, all possible experiences, of limitation.*

It would be difficult for any one of you to observe her and know, to understand, what she was going through. This is because she had to build the bridge in such a way as to leave the game intact. Thus, she looked like a normal game player, and played by all the rules of the game – while energetically, emotionally, she was going through a great deal more.

This was her purpose. This ability is a reflection of her core frequency. Though difficult, at times excruciating, and extremely challenging – as your beliefs of limitation would demand it to be – she was destined to be victorious.

And she was. She built a bridge – piece by piece, belief by belief – to more and more expansive beliefs, out of the egg. Until one day, the delicate thread emerged, and from all of *us*, there was great rejoicing.

In that moment of connection, we were able to finally, finally, finally perceive and understand all that you have been experiencing by way of these wavelengths. These vast oceans of beliefs, of lifetimes, were perceptible by us. And you were too! We could finally see you, and connect with you, energetically again.

But manifestations were still far from being possible. Her work was not done. She continued to build the bridge to what you might call "higher and higher" wavelengths. And through this process, a great many were able to connect to, to understand, your vast experience of limitation. That connection, that understanding, has been a blessing to many. *What you have created here has been a blessing to many.*

And each time she built connections to higher and higher wavelengths, part of that energy was naturally, by way of the bridge, accessible to any who had chosen to participate within the egg. She brought all of this back down to Earth, as you might say.

Was she conscious of what she was building? Only partially, for if she had become completely conscious of this, her consciousness would, by definition, be beyond the limits of the 5 Senses Spectrum. And then, as we have described, she would have become imperceptible to you. For if one does not align completely to your wavelengths of limitation, they are out of the game. Thus she was, for a number of years, torn between two worlds: the wavelengths of expansive love and light in which we exist, and the wavelengths of limitation in which you have been residing.

This masterpiece that you hold in your hands is a composite of wavelengths. Today, it may feel like a singular tone or voice. As your consciousness expands, what you will begin to recognize – across energetic experiences – is more and more nuanced. You would be able to read this book and "hear" within the words a variety of perspectives that combine into this reflection of what you are experiencing. Our voices, her voice, are all combined here.

Why is this important?

Because it can reach to *all* of your wavelengths of limitation. Some of you will resonate more easily with certain messages in these pages than others. That is natural. For you will choose, you will navigate, into the light, by however it works best for the evolution of *your own beliefs*.

Remember, your BSC is a vast, colossal, dynamic, and evolving creation. There is no one path that would work for all. This delicate strand of light on which you now stand is actually a combination of many, many ribbons of light to which the Bridge Builder has connected. It is all right if some of these concepts appeal to you more than others. In fact, we would suggest that you may celebrate that! It is your growing perception of your own ability to navigate energy coming through to you by way of preference!

Are some of these beliefs "higher" than others?

Are these ribbons of light of "higher" frequency than yours?

Beloved, here we must tell you that ***there is no hierarchy.***

Hierarchy is a concept of *this egg*, of this bubble, of this BSC. It was needed, by your limited mind, in order to make sense of the environment in which you existed. Incapacitated from navigating through infinite wavelengths, it reduced and defined what you would navigate through by using the concepts of "better" and "worse." This idea of a scale is completely, perfectly a reflection of your chosen experience of limitation.

There is not a single belief, in all of creation, that is better or worse than any other. They are just different ways of experiencing energy.

And your preference for a belief over another is not an indication of fundamental value, or better-ness, of that belief. It is simply your growing ability to perceive differences in energy and sense your own path of greatest expansion.

We understand. You may feel the action of the belief system telling you that we are of "higher" realms and more expanded perspective. Clearly, this is "better" than your limited perspective. The Bridge Builder is now of higher realms as well, she must be more amazing, more powerful, more capable.

But Beloved, could you not sense an equally valid viewpoint that says we simply hold a different perspective? We simply experience different wavelengths of energy. Your Bridge Builder simply has different capabilities. And you have different capabilities from all of us.

Your ideas in the deficiencies, the subservience of humanity, have served you well in this experience of limitation. But they are needed no longer.

Humanity is as special, as gloriously unique, as capable, as powerful, as *any other being, on any other wavelength, in all of creation.*

We are not more special than you are. We are equals.

You are not more special than another human, beast, bird, or bug. You are equals.

We are not more special than another human, beast, bird, or bug! They are our equal.

Energetically, there is no hierarchy. There is simply the vast, infinite, contrasting experiences of different wavelengths of light.

And what you prefer, across it all.

Mass Consciousness

Early on, in her conscious connection to us, the Bridge Builder gave us a name: The Chorus. Though she was delighted in how we celebrated how perfectly that name suited us, it would be many more months, even years, before she would understand how rightly she had chosen.

What she was already beginning to sense were her growing connections to a great variety of representatives from a great variety of different wavelengths of light.

All of us reside outside of your egg. All of us hail from different bubbles of light.

We would describe our bubbles as being different Belief System Complexes (BSCs). Please understand, however, that here your squeaks and whistles run out of capacity to describe the differences in experience by way of *all* of these BSCs. Our experiences of beliefs are *vastly* different than yours. Your experience of beliefs has been wholly limiting. It is possible, quite possible, to experience beliefs that are perpetually expansive!

Our bubbles are fluid and evolving, just like yours. Sometimes our bubbles overlap with other belief systems, or delicately connect, the way we are all doing here via the Bridge of Light.

In the early days, before the Bridge Builder's consciousness had expanded, we each were given the opportunity to connect to your conscious limitation. Through her eyes, through her vibration, we understood all that you have created here. It is a marvel!

Energetically, when you connect to another being, their entire resonance is conveyed in an instant. The concepts of partial understanding, of being able to deceive or hide portions of yourself, etc., are purely fabrications of this egg. And what an experience *that* is, we would say! Thus, once we were able to connect to you via your Bridge Builder energetically, we understood, we resonated, with *all* of you in an instant. Those frequencies became a resonant part of our entire chord of frequencies, of our entire being. Like an instant upload to our database, you might say.

However, your consciousness, through the choice to have the experience of awakening, has chosen not to do the instant upload thing. You will gradually, lovingly, consciously, expand to awareness of all that you have experienced here and all that there will be to experience "out there." Else you would miss out on the "awakening." (Trust us, you don't want to miss out on that!)

Would you consider any one of our bubbles, our Belief System Complexes (BSCs), to be a different dimension?

In actuality, that is up to you.

But allow us to share our perspective.

As we have reviewed in the first part of this book, your 5 Senses BSC is a colossal and vast creation of the experience of wavelengths of limitation that disallow the newness, the naturally inherent creative power of energy. Your perception of these wavelengths is what you call your emotions. This creation is immense, and you have spent many lifetimes experiencing different portions, different areas of this BSC.

You now know that time, distance, and your body are part of the setup of your BSC and are not fundamental to creation. But they do dictate, both consciously and unconsciously, how you experience "reality" – that is, your perception of energies.

We have already reviewed your concept of dimension, let us now add to it by reviewing what it means to be "physical."

Today, we would suggest that your definition of physical – as is the case with mind and consciousness, reality, and dimension – largely overlaps with what you perceive via the 5 Senses Spectrum. A "physical" experience simply means one in which you perceive the energies by way of your bodies. And your bodies are the resulting manifestation of your limited 5 Senses belief systems. As we have suggested before, if your beliefs were to change, so too would your bodies.

This becomes a chicken-and-egg kind of question – which defines the other? Is it that you experience energy physically through the 5 Senses, thus this has become your definition of reality? Or is there a fundamental construct underpinning this all which you sense as being "physical," and so assign that sensation to your experience of reality?

It would be the latter.

Allow us to explain.

We have described the 5 Senses BSC as colossal. Vast, galactic, bigger than billions of galaxies, etc.

You now know that beyond your own BSC are additional Belief System Complexes – the bubbles – fluidly dynamic and moving about in a space even broader than your own BSC.

If you were to zoom out even further, you would notice that all these Belief Systems are hanging out around, upon, within, on top of a vast composite of wavelengths. These wavelengths, compared to the infinite wavelengths of energy in creation, have a similar tone to them, a similar consistency.

This neighborhood of frequencies is what we would call a dimension.

And we would call the neighborhood of frequencies in which you find all of our BSCs, and your BSC, the Physical Dimension.

Please understand that, as usual, we are delineating between fluid constructs for the purposes of clarity. All wavelengths, all energy, is a continuum. Thus, we are artificially drawing a line at a certain point and saying here ends one thing and begins another. It would be equally valid to move that point to any place on the continuum. But for the purposes of clarification, this works well for now.

But here we must modify slightly, that is expand, your definition of "physical." For, do we have arms, legs, ears, and eyes? No. Do we believe in time and space the way you do? No. In fact, Beloved Ones, if not for your and our Bridge Builder, you would not be able to perceive us at all. We are, as you would say today, "nonphysical."

So what then makes our experience and your experience similarly "physical"? Why would we say that your bubbles and ours are in the Physical Dimension?

Good question!

This is where we must press – ever so gently, ever so slightly – on what you currently, consciously recognize. For you are *just* bringing this perception into your awareness.

How is it that much of this information feels logical to you? That a lot of it "makes sense"? That is your perception of the bridge of light. Meaning, you can resonate with these frequencies because you can resonate with everything in between. Thus, this manifests as a sensation of logic and fit. Good, you sense this.

And yet, how is it that our perspective feels completely different from yours? Or from the perspective you have been experiencing? This is your perception of the difference between our frequencies and yours. And one day you will be able to sense this difference in even more sensitive ways, picking out the different "voices" that collaborated here on these concepts. Even though what we are saying feels logical, our voice, our tone, our presence, feels *different*. Good, you sense this.

However, how is it that part of us, part of this dialogue we are having with you, feels … not incredibly different? Okay, sure, we feel more expansive or of a different perspective, but there is something familiar about us. Something attainable. Something relatable.

That Beloved, is your growing sense of the shared wavelengths on which we all resonate. The neighborhood of frequencies we call the Physical Dimension.

It is too early in your awakening to define concretely what Physical means in this context. But keep this in mind as you proceed, for what you had defined as physical overlapped heavily with your 5 Senses perception. As you expand from this perception, you will recognize that which overlapped and how it is actually much broader and much vaster.

Another term for Physical Dimension is one you have heard before: Mass Consciousness.

Now that you have this context, it is easy for us to suggest that what you had previously considered the Mass Consciousness might have been limited to your 5 Senses BSC. Is that correct? You had and have a sense of agreement with all those around you whom you perceive. And this is accurate. However, as you expand in your perception, so too does your awareness of the vastness of what these perceptions indicated. Your Mass Consciousness extends throughout your BSC – to actors and other game players whom you do not yet even consciously recollect – to our BSCs, and to many, many others.

We are all of a shared Mass Consciousness. That, Beloved, is why we can feel so different and yet so relatable at the same time.

Shall we put this in energetic terms? Yes, let us do so.

Earlier we suggested that when you resonate with a frequency you are in alignment with it. Said another way, you are agreeing to it.

All players of your game have aligned to your frequencies of limitation, and in so doing agree to the rules of your game. Those agreements manifested at their core as the concepts of finiteness and insufficiency. These concepts, these tenets, then beget further manifestation that you call your beliefs about time, distance, and body. And those beget more limiting beliefs such as prevention and protection and so on. Down, down, down into the depths of limitation.

But at the heart of it, resonance is agreement. Agreement is resonance.

When you zoom out – further, further, further – and look down on your BSCs (the 5 Senses BSC and the New BSC), and all of our BSCs, and see how closely they swirl around together, you might recognize that that proximity floats atop underlying wavelengths of energy. We have named this composite of wavelengths (artificially delineated from those on either side) the Physical Dimension.

Thus, even from within your BSC, you are also resonating within this composite of frequencies, are you not?

Thus, you are agreeing to them, correct?

Thus, we are all agreeing to *something?* Underneath all our vast, individual, expansive experiences, across all these many and myriad BSCs, we share a frequency.

We would suggest, Beloved Ones, that none among you has a conscious experience of leaving the Physical Dimension.

You are most often recalling, or reconnecting to, experiences of energy within your own BSC. Other times, other places, other lifetimes, as you would say, and bringing those into your expanding consciousness.

Until the Bridge of Light, you had been unable to connect to anything outside of your BSC, else you would have violated the agreements of your BSC. You would have ostensibly ejected yourself from the game.

Can you leave the Physical Dimension? Of course!

By virtue of the continuum of all energy, all dimensions naturally connect to all others. You may pass on to any other frequencies at your leisure.

However, given your current *position* – to use your terminology – it is highly improbable (though not impossible) that you would vibrate to a frequency that is of something other than the Physical Dimension, today.

Again, to use your terminology of location, you are at the heart of the Physical Dimension. You are at the center. You are at the greatest depths of limitation. You are the utmost, the leading edge, the creative force behind these frequencies. You are at the apex of creation. You are the driver, the generator, the tip of the arrow that plunges into these frequencies of physicality. So much more so than any of us. So much more so than any who revel in, who enjoy, who experience this Mass Consciousness and this Physical Dimension.

Perhaps this puts your concepts – your judgments, your beliefs – about humanity, and all your many limitations, into a new light.

THE PHYSICAL DIMENSION

By some definitions, a dimension is a composite of a variety of energetic wavelengths more closely bound by momentum and participation.

Those who agree to participate in a dimension, participate in its creation.

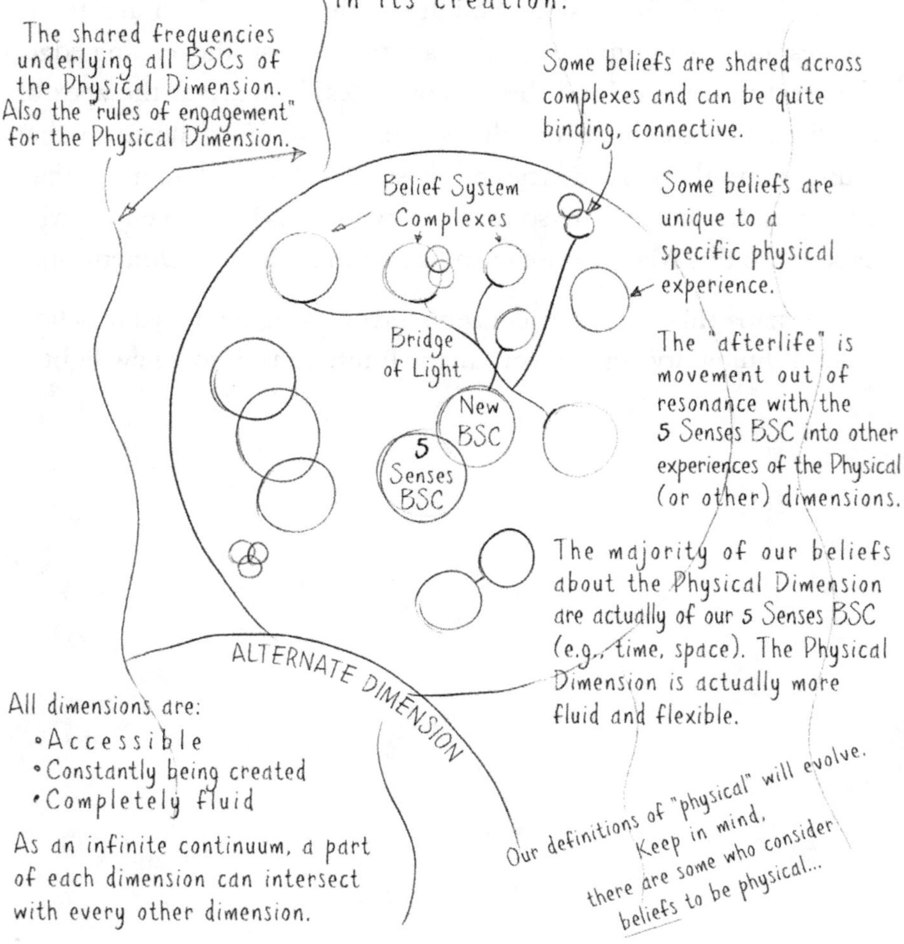

The shared frequencies underlying all BSCs of the Physical Dimension. Also the "rules of engagement" for the Physical Dimension.
Some beliefs are shared across complexes and can be quite binding, connective.
Belief System Complexes
Some beliefs are unique to a specific physical experience.
Bridge of Light
New BSC
5 Senses BSC
The "afterlife" is movement out of resonance with the 5 Senses BSC into other experiences of the Physical (or other) dimensions.
The majority of our beliefs about the Physical Dimension are actually of our 5 Senses BSC (e.g., time, space). The Physical Dimension is actually more fluid and flexible.
ALTERNATE DIMENSION
All dimensions are:
•Accessible
•Constantly being created
•Completely fluid
As an infinite continuum, a part of each dimension can intersect with every other dimension.
Our definitions of "physical" will evolve. Keep in mind, there are some who consider beliefs to be physical...

By way of participating in the 5 Senses BSC, we had agreed NOT to perceive these things.

(*All of this is fluid, dynamic, and evolving.)

Illustration 22: The Physical Dimension

Chapter 11

Humanity

So much you have learned, Beloved! So much expansion of consciousness, manifesting as these words! You are understanding so much more than just chapters ago. And so now, finally, finally we can ask an important question, and this question will have a great deal more meaning to you than it could have before.

What, exactly, does it mean to be *human?*

Is it the definition of the physical instrument you created to experience these wavelengths? Is it simply the limitations of your 5 Senses? Is that body you can look down upon right now, what you would call *human?*

Is it any and all who participate in your particular BSC? Which would mean, all you are capable of perceiving, from neighbors to bears to spiders? Are they all, technically, human?

Is it any and all who participate in the Physical Dimension? Could we be *human* too?!

Such fantastic questions! Such immense and expansive thinking from where you were just a little bit ago.

And we are gleeful, we are revelrous, to be able to explore this with you. For by these understandings, so much *love* will pour into your experience. So much flowing of energy as you have ever yet consciously known.

Beloved, it is time.

In actuality, you may choose any of the above to be your definition of the word "human." We are now touching down to energies that are very close, very much at play, with the energies of your BSC. Thus, these are your beliefs to build.

But, as usual, we will share our perspective with you, and you may take any of it into your frequencies that pleases you.

We would suggest that the mind-body instrument via which you experience your day-to-day life falls short of the definition of human. That is but the naming of a very specific manifestation. It might be appropriate to simply name this manifestation humanoid. Is your body instrument the definition of all that you are as a human? Of all that you feel, dream, imagine, and create? We do not think so.

To be human has far, far more to do with everything you have experienced, and built, by way of your lifetimes in this vast BSC. Though you have taken different manifested forms in this environment over the many billions of years of your participation, you have always been *human*. You have lived *a human existence*, be it in the humanoid form you know today, or not.

Your definition of "like kind" is expanding. Today, you use your 5 Senses to determine who is like you. You use this to study and define your concept of species. You use it to look at birds and beasts and bugs and bacteria of your planet and say, "These are like me, and those are not." This limited perception of yourselves, and of reality, has manifested millennia of apparent isolation and loneliness. You perceive little. And what little you perceive you judge to be different, and thus manifest a dwindled connection to all other life you encounter.

You have spent a great many millennia in the experience you call "alone."

And this experience was desired, and this experience was perfect.

However, Beloved, we must say to you that, just like control, and just like trust, you must create the experience of alone. *You created the experience of lack of others of like kind.* You narrowed your definitions to civilizations, to societies, to tribes, and, finally, to families. In actuality, you define very few as *truly* being of like kind. And no more so than in your current epoch, where everyone seems to hold different beliefs than you, and everyone seems perhaps difficult to trust completely. A chosen few, a chosen very few out of the universe of infinite beings, do you feel truly understand you and connect to you.

Isolation and loneliness are not the way of the universe.

You are *surrounded* by those who are of like kind to you. Your universe is teeming with life who share a common bond with you. Your uniqueness will forever and always be truly unique. Your Core Frequency is inviolable no matter with which BSC you choose to resonate. Yet you will find, as you move forward, greater and more powerful ways of relating, of connecting, to beings and life that you previously felt were so different as to be unreachable.

Your trees are alive and conscious in a way that is vastly different from yours, yet still, in many ways, play by the rules of the game. You will delight in discovering how they have done so, and what their experience *of you* has been. And you will discover, you will expand into the conscious awareness that trees are actually *so much more* than the leaves and twigs you currently perceive on the 5 Senses Spectrum!

Your animals are also conscious. In a variety of delightful ways! They experience reality with such nuance as will bring to light the uniqueness of all that you have been in your humanoid form, and the beauty of all you have experienced.

Your mountains are conscious. They are of a form, of a type of being, that is vastly expansive. That underlines much of the structure of your reality in this BSC. And they, too, expand beyond the limitations of this BSC to the beyond, just like you are doing now! Yes, there are beings who are capable of spanning multiple bubbles, of course. There are no limits in all of creation. In this way, they are bridges as well. They will reflect much to you.

In each of these examples – mountains, animals, trees – you simply have been unable to reach, to connect, to their consciousness because they were ever so slightly outside the rules of your game. Had you been able to chat with the mountains in the same way you can your next door neighbor, your experience of isolation would have been vastly reduced!

Beloved, from our vantage point, **all who participate in this most incredible, limited, expansive 5 Senses BSC are what we call *human*.**

We know, this is a change of thinking for you. Does this mean that a lion, a deer, or a moose could be considered human? If you can perceive them from your current conscious perspective, from within the 5 Senses BSC, is there a part of them that is playing your game? That is "human"? You will find out, Beloved! For as you begin to expand in your perception of self, you will find that your definitions of self also expand. Where once you defined yourselves by your arms, legs, your DNA, your methods of communication, these things will begin to fall away in importance as you recognize the energetic underpinnings of your kind. You will discover new things, new aspects, and apply new words to them. And in those discoveries – which span beyond much more than the 5 Senses – you will recognize the shared traits you have with others. And you will be able to connect to them via those shared traits. In so doing, suddenly a tiger will not be *so* different from you. Beloved, trees are not very different from you either. You do perceive them in your game after all, do you not? They are playing too!

There are so many more of you than you yet realize, than you could yet know. You are just beginning to emerge from your shell of isolation, a shell that we might suggest existed even within this limiting shell of your BSC! For there are those within your BSC who were aware of each other, who interacted with each other, slightly more so than you do in your current incarnation today.

Thus we must term you, the you who believes you are of this time and of this place, and disconnected from other life, an *Earthling*. But this is just a name for a manifestation. The same way humanoid is. It has very little to do with the energetic underlying structure of what you are experiencing – it is the end result. The combination of beliefs in time, place, finiteness, and insufficiency, worked out as being a humanoid, living on the planet Earth, in the year 20XX. That, Beloved, is the definition of Earthling.

But do you feel how much more you are by being *human?*

Do you feel a growing connection to *all others* who participate here? How you all, collectively, are humanity? The driving force behind this most expansive, most amazing BSC.

HUMAN

What does it mean to be human?

Today

This concept is based on the limits of the 5 Senses.
You designate "human" based on what you can see, and beliefs about what it should "look like," which actually alters what you see.
There are many humans who do not look human to you. Or whom you do not yet even perceive.

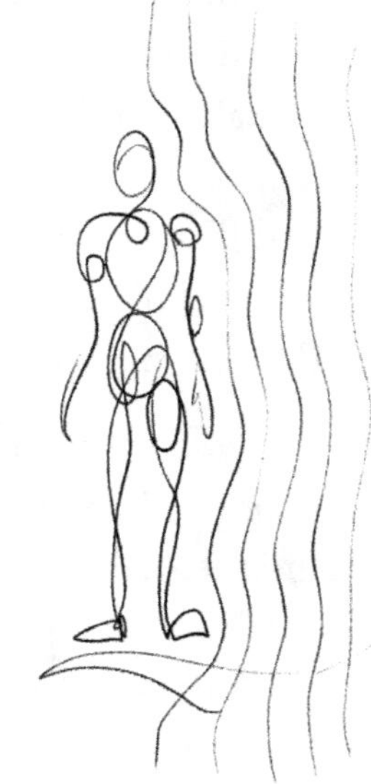

Expanded

This concept may be based on an expanded field of perception.

As you expand into yourselves, you experience growing unification across your parts.
This will be reflected in a growing sense of unification with ALL life.
The concept of species BROADENS.

What does the neighborhood of frequencies of human represent?

The way you feel when you are not being held down, artificially, by belief systems of lack and limitation, is the closest proxy you have to knowing what this human frequency feels like.
This is who you are.

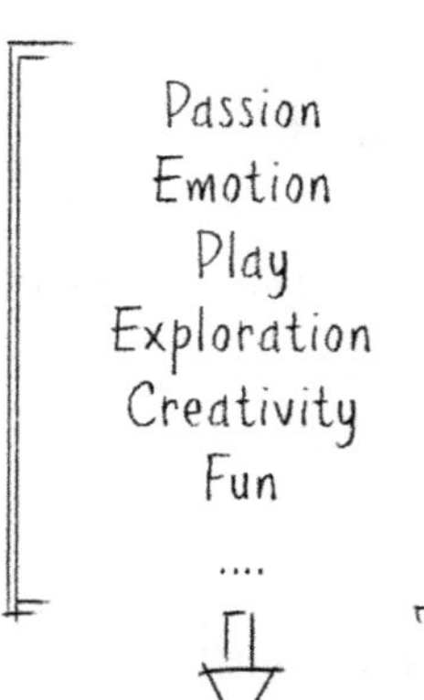

Such limited words for such VAST frequencies that surround your CORE FREQUENCY.

Those who hale of these frequencies are of "your kind" whether they "look" human or not!

YOUR FAMILY IS FAR MORE VAST THAN YOU CAN IMAGINE.

Illustration 23: Human

Group Reality

In all this conversation we reached "up" to very high levels of energy and wound down, down, down to your current frequencies. To this point, we have stepped very lightly around what we might call "individual" beliefs. For, in so doing, we are creating a manifestation right now, are we not? And in your perception of manifestation you will build new beliefs. And there is no set of beliefs in all of your BSC that are more super-charged than your individual beliefs because *those are the beliefs you are currently activating.*

At the individual level, there is a part of you that is building the New BSC and a part that is still in the 5 Senses BSC, and both will build beliefs by way of this manifestation. *Thus, you will feel both as you read these words – an enlightenment, a release, an ease, as well as disallowance, resistance, and limitation.*

There is nothing wrong with either sensation! It is simply your read of the energies. Your preference for the one over the other is telling you in which direction the path of greatest expansion calls you. You are flowing in that direction effortlessly. There is nothing you need "do," other than celebrate this growing perception.

Perhaps by now you have picked up on the idea that your BSC, all BSCs, and energy in general are rather complex, fluid, and, we might even say, layered. In an infinite continuum in all directions.

We would like to give you two ways of understanding this with regard to your current resonance.

Option 1:

Energy Flowing into Your BSC (aka Layers)

The first is via the concept of energy coming "in" to your egg.

The pure light of creation passes through a first layer of beliefs, which here are what you call finiteness and insufficiency. We would call this first layer the primary. All players receive energy through the primary layer of a BSC, thus all players within your BSC experience *in some way* finiteness and insufficiency. It is the main objective of this game.

Once the energy passes through the primary, it passes through the next layer, which we generally classified for you as the beliefs about time, distance, and body. The vast majority of players reside within this layer, thus all experience *some version* of time, distance, and body.

Is there a small space between the primary and the next layer of beliefs? Yes.

Are there players who resonate out there, and though experience finiteness and insufficiency, are not subject to beliefs about time, distance, and body? Yes. This is a vast and dynamic BSC. Players may experience any or all of the layers.

Moving "deeper" into the BSC, we hit the next layer of energy, which we would loosely classify as beliefs in (lack of) control. Those players within this layer experience *some version* of lack of control, though these may vary.

Beloved, this may go on and on for quite a few layers. And while we seem to be doing pretty well in simplifying a galactic, dynamic, billions-of-times-per-second changing BSC, it would still take us only a few million more years to truly describe all the detail therein.

Thus, we jump ahead. Many, many layers deep, far away from where the energy first entered, lie two closely and dynamically intertwined layers we would call "group" beliefs and "individual" beliefs. For the sake of simplicity, we will just call them group beliefs. The players herein participate in a kind of strict limitation with other members of a defined group. When the group beliefs shift, their beliefs shift. If the group doesn't allow a belief, they don't believe it. If the group manifests a new belief, they believe it. These beliefs, of course, trickle down to, or affect, beliefs about each individual – their worthiness, if their desires are allowable, what actions they may take, etc.

You, Beloved, are reaching us from all the way down in this very specific, very limiting frequency of group belief. You would define your group as those around you who share this resonance. By way of these beliefs, you all look a lot alike. You act alike, you communicate alike, you think alike, you behave alike, you react alike, you eat alike, etc. You have named this resonance "species."

The way these players energize the group agreement is what defines, is what creates, your shared reality (that is, perception of energy).

Option 2:

Energy Flowing Through Your Resonance (aka Ribbons)

Another, equally valid perspective about how this works could be described by ribbons of light, much how, we earlier suggested, your Bridge of Light was constructed.

Rather than beginning by imagining energy coming "in" to your BSC, let us try a different approach. Let us imagine that the energy of life and all creation pours through you. It begins within you.

You look out onto all creation, and you see a beautiful ribbon of light – and, for the purposes of making this example more visceral, we will also say sound. You have never heard this type of note before. You have a desire to experience it. You move toward the ribbon of light and begin to resonate with it. We would call this ribbon "finiteness and insufficiency."

Soon you are joined by many, many other beings, and all of you are resonating with this frequency and energizing it. Experiencing this delightful, unique, vastly expansive sound.

As you resonate with this ribbon of light, you notice that it is actually made up of three different interwoven ribbons. Each a note of beauty that contributes to the main note of the primary ribbon of light. From a certain vantage point, you could say that each of these three ribbons is its own, stand-alone note in all of creation. From another equally valid vantage point, you could say that these ribbons are but "sub-ribbons" of the primary ribbon of finiteness and insufficiency. Let us continue with this latter concept.

Some of the other beings – the other players of this note – decide to continue vibrating with all three, with the whole thing. You, however, decide to move deeper into the notes. Your consciousness focuses down on the deepest of the three notes. Technically, you are still vibrating with, and within, the entire chord, but have chosen to focus on the experience of one of the three main notes.

Other players move to resonate with the other notes. Some join you on your note.

As you vibrate with this note, you realize that it, too, is made up of different ribbons of light, finer and more narrow. You are fascinated by one in particular. You move your consciousness down further, into a focused experience of this note.

And on, and on, and on.

Sometimes you move back up between ribbons – between notes. Sometimes you move laterally across ribbons, across notes. You spent millennia exploring and experiencing all the notes, the finer levels of light, that make up this primary ribbon that is finiteness and insufficiency. Or what we generally classify as disallowance. You might say that "lifetimes" are experienced throughout this ribbon of light.

We would suggest that one way to think about your current "position" within this ribbon – this vast Belief System Complex of dynamic, flowing, changing, and vast levels of ribbons – is that you are down, down, down on a very specific, very deep note. You are thus subject to all that you are still resonating with, all the frequencies of the larger ribbons within which this sub-, sub-, sub-ribbon is resonating – finiteness, insufficiency, time, distance, body, lack of control, and so on – but your consciousness is focused on this particular note.

This note represents a resonance of very specific, very limiting experience. This has manifested as what you would call a "group reality." Players of this note will resonate with – that is, agree to – its limitations. Thus all will manifest *some version* of a shared, consistent, cyclical, limiting perception of energy, which is what you call reality.

We call this sub-, sub-, sub-, sub-ribbon the 5 Senses BSC.

AWAKENING

Two (among an infinite number of) ways to visualize your energetic position and expansion. We consider this entire collection of layers, or notes, within the Primary of Finiteness and Insufficiency, the 5 Senses BSC, named for your position in it from which you perceived our consciousness.

You might decide to name each layer or note. You might decide to name the collection of layers/notes something else? Up to you! These are your beliefs to build!

Option 1, LAYERS: Energy Flowing Into Your BSC

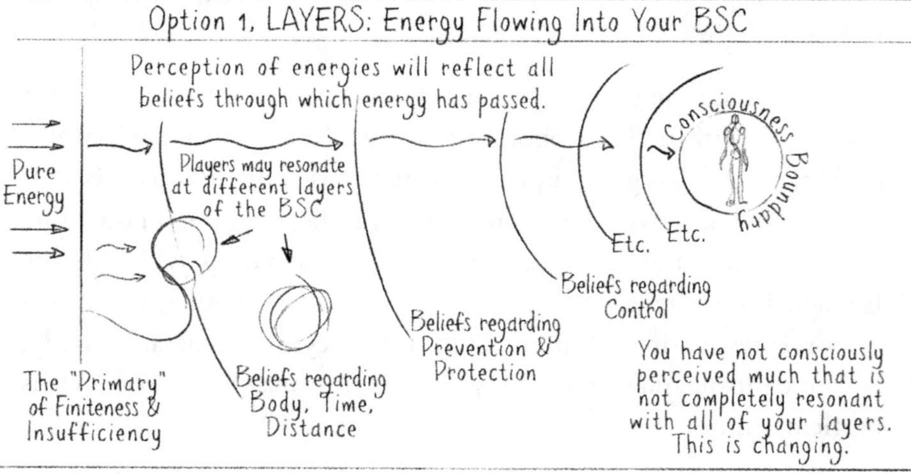

Option 2, RIBBONS : Energy Flowing Through Your Resonance

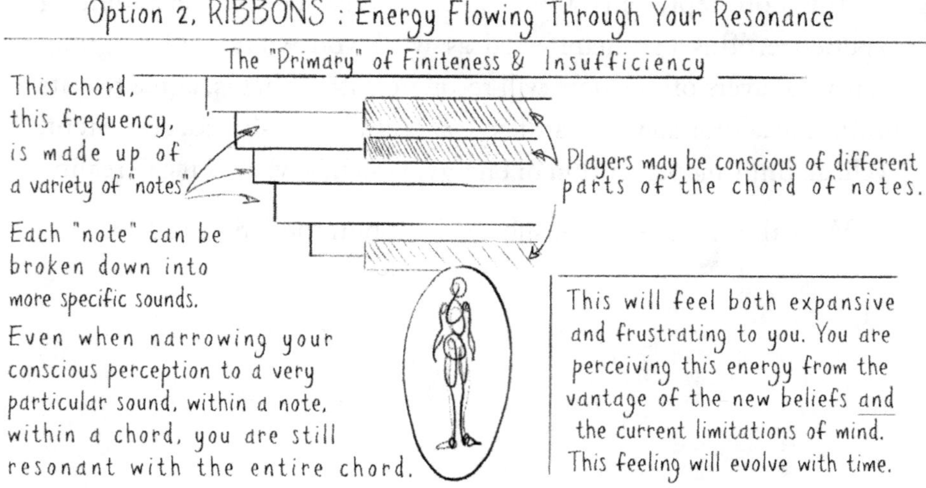

The "Primary" of Finiteness & Insufficiency
This chord, this frequency, is made up of a variety of "notes"
Players may be conscious of different parts of the chord of notes.
Each "note" can be broken down into more specific sounds.
Even when narrowing your conscious perception to a very particular sound, within a note, within a chord, you are still resonant with the entire chord.
This will feel both expansive and frustrating to you. You are perceiving this energy from the vantage of the new beliefs and the current limitations of mind. This feeling will evolve with time.

Illustration 24: Awakening

Intuition

Did we just flip everything on its head? Did we just make it overly complicated? Is it bubbles or layers or ribbons or light? Did you feel like you knew which one came first and then second, or was on top and then under, and now you are not so sure? Does your brain "hurt" a little bit?

That sensation is, currently, your conscious perception of the edges of this particular note – that is, your current belief systems. It is the boundary between what your consciousness has been resonating with and the new beliefs, the new resonances, which you are expanding toward.

Your belief systems – or said another way, your mind – demand answers within the confines of the existing structure. Your mind wants answers about these more expansive frequencies constrained down into your *very specific* concepts of body, time, distance, and so on.

Thus, mind will want to know the shape of these things: are these bubbles or ribbons? How do they compare in size or shape?

Mind will want to know the distance and space of these things: which one is the largest? Are the smaller ones within or beside the bigger ones?

Mind will want to know which is better and which is worse: are we of "higher" energies and you of "lower"?

Mind will want to know time and order: did the lifetimes of experiencing other ribbons, other portions of your BSC, happen already, or not yet? Or is time a giant loop (like you view much of your existence as cyclical and repeating, we might point out!)?

Do you feel it, Beloved? Do you sense the "complexity" of what we are describing? That sensation of brain's immense exertion of energy into limitation? This is the point at which in a conversation with another that you might "space out," only to come back a moment later and say, "Sorry, what did you just say? I must have missed that." This is the point, when listening to a detailed lecture or speech, that you start daydreaming. This is the experience of reading a lengthy article on a particular topic, only to notice that your eyes continued to scan multiple paragraphs, but your "mind" wasn't present in the same way.

"I do that all the time," you say. "What *is* that?" you say.

It is the boundary between your old 5 Senses BSC and your New BSC. It is the energetic difference between this very deep layer inside your egg, and the more expansive layer "above" you. It is the difference in resonance between this ribbon of light, this note, and the addition – the expansion to – notes around you.

This is *the experience of conscious awakening.*

You are not as enmeshed in Mind, in these beliefs, as you once were. Your *focus* is softening, your *attention* is expanding. You are not as narrow, as specific, as limited as you once were. Your presence in the busy business of mind is softening.

Beloved, you did not miss anything in those conversations, lectures, or articles. Rather for a moment, your consciousness became broader, and you were experiencing vaster energies. If you will notice, you were still engaging in conversation, still "listening" or still "reading." However, at some point you noticed – you judged – that you had not been doing so in the same way. That point is the moment that you snap back into the dynamic action of this BSC and your beliefs cause you to ask, "Where was I?"

When your Bridge Builder built the Bridge of Light, she built it from way, way, way down in your BSC bubble, from the most sub of sub-ribbons, all the way out to us, who are beyond the ribbon, the boundary, of finiteness and insufficiency. Meaning, we resonate in a different way, in a different place. We do not have the beliefs about finiteness and insufficiency the same way you do.

Many of us were given the opportunity to communicate with the Bridge Builder from her conscious perspective of your great limitation before her consciousness began to expand. We were able to reflect this to her, and through her work of the bridge she was able to receive this knowing, but that was the extent of it. She was still very much an Earthling human connecting to us.

In an instant, we were able to energetically identify all that she is, all that you all are, and all that you have experienced. However, we were delighted to experience with her the way in which her consciousness – that is, your belief systems – limit all that is.

To be more specific, she began by asking us what would seem to be pertinent questions.

"Where are you?"

What a question! We marveled! A "where"? What an amazing concept! We replied by explaining to her that we do not share her concepts of place, distance, or space.

"What do you look like?"

"Look" and "like"? What a miraculous creation! That your energy, your existences, could be narrowed down into such specific manifestations? And that you identify each other by your *similarities*? We replied by explaining to her that we do not share her beliefs in bodies, in instruments. We are nonphysical, where physical is defined by your 5 Senses!

"Are you benevolent, are you loving, are you of higher realms?"

In an instant we recognized that by your beliefs then, there could be encounters and experiences of others that you would judge to be malevolent, unloving, or of "lower" energies. Even more critically, that by her beliefs *she* could not perceive these things on her own and had to collect manifestations in order to determine if we were trustworthy, including giving us the opportunity to speak for ourselves. Incredible! Absolutely incredible! To which we assured her that we are loving, that she had reached a wavelength of love, and by that definition there could be none she would encounter who could be "unloving" on this wavelength.

She sent us appreciation, but also noted – in an energetic way – that she wasn't so naive as to believe the "voices in her head" when they said, "Don't worry! We're trustworthy!" To which we replied, gleefully, "Play the game!"

And boy, did she! She put us through every sort of test imaginable, determined to not let us "through" to her kind until she knew with certainty that we would bring only love to your reality. It would be many, many months before she truly trusted us.

Eventually, as you can imagine, the Bridge Builder ran out of questions. There were just no more 5 Senses queries she could make that she had not done already, or that were not nullified by her growing awareness of the differences in our existences. It was only then, after much manifestation and building beliefs to support the Bridge of Light, that she was able to begin to allow in new understandings. In that moment, she began to receive the experience of our perspective, of our frequencies, the same way we had received of her in an instant.

If your current mental frameworks are insufficient to consciously understand the next levels of the game, you see now why the building of new beliefs is so invaluable. Said another way, because you are expanding, the manifested beliefs that will result are inevitable. As are the other manifestations beyond just thoughts and beliefs, those all-important tools and abilities of which we have spoken, via which you perceive and will navigate broader frequencies.

Your emotional array.

Imagination.

Inspiration.

Attention.

Trust.

And before we close this immense work, we will leave you with one more.

Intuition.

What else could intuition be but an energetic perception of frequencies *prior to their reflection* in 5 Senses manifestation? What you call intuition, a knowing, a "feeling," has been perceived by you, yet there is not often a matching indication in your waking life. Often, for those of you who have more practice with intuition, there is not yet even a conceived thought. It is pre-mind, outside of mind, that is, **the sensation of frequencies that have not yet been molded by this 5 Senses BSC.**

You will now recognize in the sense of an intuition a similarity to the sense of an inspiration or of a desire.

An intuition will tell you what is coming.

An inspiration will tell you where to go.

A desire will advise you of where you are headed.

As your consciousness expands beyond the 5 Senses BSC, you will find that the immense action of these beliefs soften. Thus, when you receive an intuition, inspiration, or desire, they will be able to persist for longer durations of time before they are judged, or narrowed, into something specific that is acceptable to the 5 Senses field of play. In that growing space of allowance, more about that energy will come through to you. Though they may feel very intangible today, your perceptions of these – and many other things – will grow.

In Love

Our most Beloved, most cherished ones, there are not enough words, in any of your languages, that could describe, that could reach the levels of love we feel for you. For what you have created here, for all that you are, for all that you share with us. For you.

You and we, right now, are on the wavelength of love. And you may reach this frequency any time. And in the reaching for it, energetically you attain it. You do not need to "feel" love, you do not need any manifestation on the 5 Senses wavelengths to validate what you have done. As an energetic being, "reaching" for something is your choice to resonate with it.

Reach for love anytime, and you are instantly here, with us.

We are always with you.

Enjoy this process. Enjoy this unfolding. Enjoy each step you take on the Bridge of Light. Marvel at all that creation has given you in this experience. Just as we marvel at all of you, all of the time.

This is but a beautiful, glorious beginning.

May you recognize each day, and in all aspects of yourself, the light that you radiate.

We will speak with you again, very soon.

Chapter 12

The Bridge Builder

There is a reason you are hearing from me at the end of this book.

Several, in fact.

We began these chapters on the broadest frequencies, you might say, and became more narrow – that is, closer to our wavelengths – as we went along. So it makes sense that the last chapter is actually your energetically closest chapter, from your fellow human. (Hello there, nice to meet you.)

Also, in hearing from "just me" at the end of the book, after having consumed the rest of it, you will begin to recognize my voice, and will see how it was represented. This will help you in bringing to consciousness your ability to hear different voices – perceptions of different energies – in a combined work. This is an important experience.

Finally, this chapter is about integration. In your reading of this entire work, you vibrated with a whole lot of different energies.

The frequency of this chapter is your time, your space, to begin plugging those energies into your current frequencies. The Chorus calls this "walking the bridge." I like to think you are building the bridge, too.

So, human party at the back of the bus. You ready?

Let's do this.

Awakening Is a Giant Pain in the Ass and Also It's the Most Amazing Thing

I could tell you about the decades of my spiritual quests. The piles of self-help books and yogic texts, my trials of everything from Baptism to Buddhism, the hilariously unsuccessful meditations and the terrifyingly successful ones, the nights attempting to teach myself physics, and the transformative experiences of hearing channeled works. Or we can just skip to the part where things got real.

One night it occurred to me that I could attempt my own connection. Being human, this one thought translated into several weeks of "preparing" for (that is, slowing down) the manifestation. I ordered and read a book about how to channel. I determined my own answers to questions about how I would know if it was a "good" connection, or if I was safe. I even had a mental step-by-step process in mind.

But that's not what got me to open up. It was frustration.

One night, in a complete huff over my desire for answers that I had *still* not found, I sat down on the edge of my bathtub and opened to the connection.

I was completely stunned when I felt something there.

And not just something, a palpable being or beings, and they were elated, ebullient, ecstatic over our connection. It was like walking into the middle of raucous cheers already underway, but the reason for the raucous cheers was that I had just walked in. It was both an immense culmination of something, and also instantaneous. The logic I knew of time and order and space was broken. My mind burst into a million questions. Fear and joy erupted simultaneously in my system. Chills, shudders, and shaking swept through my body. I stopped the connection.

About a day later, I came down with a monstrous flu.

As one might imagine, while I lay there beside bottles of aspirin and glasses of water, my mind had plenty of time to obsessively churn over two questions: "What the heck was *that?*" And "Did *that* cause *this?*"

By the time I recovered, I had decided that I didn't have enough information to make a determination. I had to try again. With great trepidation and hope, I returned to the edge of the bathtub. The exact same spot on the edge of the bathtub, actually. (I hope you see the human aspect in this choice!)

After this second attempt, I got a sinus infection.

The next several years of my life were characterized by this roller coaster. Though the details evolved, the cycles were relatively the same. Extreme highs to extreme lows, back and forth, back and forth. My body deteriorated, my emotional stability crumbled, and there were days when I felt I was literally at hell's doorstep. While at the same time my knowledge accelerated, my ability to love expanded, and there were moments so divine I felt transformed into light itself.

Was I crazy to keep going? Or would I have been crazy to stop?

Beloved Ones – for yes, you are very, very beloved by me too – this is awakening. This *is* the two sides of the same coin. The perspective we are awakening to having held, by way of the perspective into which we are awakening.

You will discover, as you move forward, that these two aspects of being, of judgment, expand with you. Awakening is not the shift to a higher or better set of knowledge and existence – *it is expansion into the validity of all options*. Transcendence does not bring you to a place of more specific answers, of knowing what is truly "right." Only a constructed reality could create the illusion of such a place. Transcendence is expansion, and expansion is an evolution into the recognition that there is more than one right, more than one reality, and many ways to exist. It is expansion into choice. It is expansion into perceiving more of the infiniteness of infinite creation.

Yes, I was crazy to keep going. Yes, I would have been crazy to stop.

Both perspectives are valid.

The perspective of the five senses mind, which added up all the chills, shudders, and illness and determined that this was causal and risky, was right.

And the perspective of intuition and desire, which told me that I was ok and that this was wanted, was valid.

I was sent on a grand tour around our 5 Senses BSC and every belief of limitation. Every single step was a crossroads. In one direction, I recognized the validity of what my five senses were perceiving, in another direction was the growing validity of things they could not. Every single time, eventually, I chose the path toward things outside the spectrum of the 5 Senses. Sometimes the choice was easy, and sometimes it was excruciating.

This, they tell me, is how I built the bridge. For every limiting aspect of our BSC, I plugged in this crossroads, this alternate. Every choice I made was a manifestation in this reality, which builds a belief, which is now accessible to anyone who so chooses. The Bridge of Light is a tapestry of carefully woven threads across all our many beliefs and lives. It is available to you all. No matter where you are, no matter what you have experienced. No matter if you deem yourself to be good, average, or horrible. No matter if you are having a good day or an apocalypse. It reaches all of it.

Is this not your story as well?

Have you not encountered deteriorating health that compelled you to search for new answers? Have you not suffered great crises and challenges that also propelled you into life changes? Have you not also lost more than you can comprehend, more than you can bear, but then crossed a distance of time from those events and saw how it shifted your perspective?

We have a great many beliefs about suffering, and many of those beliefs allow in *possibility*. That all-important loophole that The Chorus spoke about. Particularly when it comes to suffering within our own bodies. When mysterious or difficult-to-pin-down ailments arise, we are able to ask ourselves, *what could it be*? And in that asking, we open the door to an expanded vantage point.

It is no coincidence that we are suffering a global pandemic as I write these words.

My friends, I do not have a halo or wings. I get angry, impatient, feisty, and mean. Sometimes I think of awful things to say and don't say them. Sometimes I say them anyway. I curse like a sailor, even in front of children. I know what it's like to hate. To hate others, to hate their opinions, to hate pollution, to hate my body. To loathe my body. To be disgusted by myself. In my mind's eye, I have beaten and abused others. I have murdered them. There is no stone of this entire BSC I have left unturned. There is no depth of the limitations of our kind that I have not passed through, sometimes on my knees. I have embodied the absolute worst of our kind.

Should I be ashamed of these moments?

What do you think?

No matter what opinion you hold of me and my actions, it is valid.

If you were to have witnessed me in any of these moments, you would have been right to feel disdain. Were you to see me scream at my husband, or my child, you would be right to condemn me. There is no perspective of me that you could hold that would not be valid.

Is that what you prefer?

To condemn me and my actions?

The choice is yours.

But before you decide, there are alternate perspectives of these events that are valid too. Should we try on a few and see how they feel?

From another view, one could say that we are able to feel these judgments because we are looking at these experiences from a new perspective. If we were wholly and perpetually absorbed in these moments, we would never be able to step back and ask ourselves if we like them or not. We would simply move from moment to moment, action to action. Currently, we look at our history and see a trajectory of trying to improve our "bad" behavior. We do not yet remember the lifetimes we spent destroying each other without feeling bad about it at all. It was "just life."

As you step slightly to the side of these actions, or rise slightly above them (whichever direction you prefer), you might be able to ask yourself, "Why am I doing this?" In that questioning, you may form opinions of the motives, and you may judge the motives. Perhaps that reason isn't enough to justify that action. Perhaps there is *never* enough of a reason to justify that action. These new beliefs were possible, were built, because of a distance between the action and the perspective of it.

By this view, we have already been awakening for a very, very long time.

By this view, disdain, condemnation, and judgment could be good things because they represent a growing body of beliefs that are slightly expanded from the conscious immersion in only the action itself.

Meaning, the disdain you feel right now, for others, is technically, expansion.

Should we try on another perspective? Let's zoom out a little further.

From another view, from that of my beloved friends in The Chorus, our hatred, disdain, and condemnation are but manifestations of a contrasting – if not *the* most contrasting – experience in all of creation. Which we built. Which has benefited not only us but has rippled throughout all frequencies for all time. That we should allow this experience – or sacrifice ourselves to it, if that's your preferred perspective – was an act of great courage, trust, and immense love.

What would you think now, if you saw me screaming in the parking lot? Am I a disgusting human being? Am I a slightly expanded disgusting human being? Am I simply embodying a colossal construct of beliefs without conscious awareness? Am I a master of creation, bringing light to greater than trillions and trillions of others by my noble contrast?

Up to you.

Each of these perspectives is an experience, which is a frequency, and there is no frequency in all of creation that is invalid.

This is what they mean when they emphasize that, to them, there is no hierarchy. They see nothing better about a caterpillar over a bird. Or of a mountain versus a toddler. Or of an alien versus a star. Because they see through all those judgments, all those evaluations, with which we resonate, closer to the pure frequency of each of these beings in each of these experiences. And to them, each one is infinitely beautiful and worthy of love.

You might have noticed lately, Beloved Ones, that our hierarchies are crumbling a bit. Sometimes people in sacred positions are worth looking up to, sometimes they turn out to be flawed. Sometimes people in positions of power demonstrate admirable leadership skills, other times they turn out to be imperfect. Sometimes people with access to great knowledge bring immense insight to our existence, and other times they are wrong. The position, the hierarchy, is starting to mean much less than the actions of the individual *in* that position. Our outrage over these shifting sands – the scandal, the criminality, the disappointments – has less to do with the sand, and more to do with the shifting. Because from one vantage point change is bad, risky, and dangerous, and from another it is good, beneficial, and full of potential.

We feel both.

We are all oscillating between these two frequencies. We are all building these connections between where we have been and where we are going. As we navigate back and forth, we are understanding what exists *across* and between these two frequencies: us.

We are beginning to ascertain that it's not all about beliefs, or the experience we are having. It is also about the uniqueness of each of us. The *you* that has chosen these wavelengths.

Emotions, preference, inspiration, intuition, and desire are the names we have given these burgeoning aspects of ourselves. We have been able to perceive this from the expanded viewpoint. As we oscillate, we experience life with them, then without them, with them, then without them, and by that contrast develop our clarity. We will get our feet under us very soon – it has already begun – and when we do, the sands will stop feeling so shifty. In fact, that shiftiness might just start to feel like flow.

Our civilization, as you have probably sensed, is on the verge of acquainting itself with beings who are not of "like kind," to use the terminology of The Chorus. Or *re*acquainting itself, depending on how you look at it. In these experiences, we will be exposed to even more and greatly diverse perspectives than ours.

Which do you think comes first, our growing *comfort* with diverse perspectives and realities, or the manifestation of the diverse perspectives and realities?

You guessed it.

As we release our grip on all the noise of different vantage points, and instead hear the clear song of our individual preferences, we will easily create the "space" to allow in the experiences of more and different vantage points. More room for your big ideas alongside mine. More abundance to share and less to squabble over. We will be able to marvel at and celebrate the differences between us, and build a co-existence we might, from a different vantage point, never have been able to dream possible. And then, collectively, we might allow ourselves to perceive something different "land" on planet Earth.

Let's return to that moment when I sat down on the bathtub.

Why was I so frustrated? That blessed sensation that finally led me to a point of overcoming my fears and saying, "Screw it, I'm just going to try it"?

I was frustrated because I was already feeling crummy. I was frustrated because already by that point, I had been struggling for years. My symptoms were inconsistent and incoherent. I had already been put on several different pills, and I had already had adverse effects. I raged against all of it, against all suffering, against the idea that any one of us here should *have* to suffer. I raged against all the years and effort I had spent trying to find an answer and still had found none that had satisfied me. Every fiber of my being wanted to understand *why*. I sat down on the tub, and there they were.

So did the channeling that night cause my flu, or was I already coming down with it?

Up to you.

Over the next several years, my symptoms only got worse, and my spiritual connections only grew stronger. Until such a point that I knew I could go no further spiritually nor physically – where I could not achieve a vaster frequency, nor make my own meals, nor shuffle around the cul-de-sac without someone holding my arm. Were those manifestations opening the doorway for the energetic connections, perhaps a requisite process based on my ability to play by the rules of our game? Is that why we often say, "Things get worse before they get better"?

Up to you.

When I look out at the sea of frequencies just beside us, I see beings that I previously might have considered so different than myself. Now I realize that they, too, are limited to "five senses" – though some of their senses may be different than mine, or I might count slightly more of them, the fundamental frequency is the same. We are together in this game.

When I look just beyond them, I see beings of lesser restriction who perceive so much more than I do. Yet they have powerful and even acute experiences of prevention and protection, just like me.

Beyond them I see the most dazzling beings I could have ever imagined who are unrestricted by senses or bodies or even time. Still, they experience finiteness in their way.

And beyond them, far away to the horizon, are the members of The Chorus, having their grand celebration, the way they always do. Looking back at me, at us, with reverence, awe, and love.

I know what I prefer.

There is just one more thing I must tell you for now, and that is this: there has always been a bridge. I have always been here, with you. This has always been my role. There is no "down" into the depths of this limiting experience and then crawling our way out of it. There is only through. You and I have been on this bridge the entire time. You were never bridge-less, though for a time we gave ourselves the experience of seeming so. We were always destined to emerge victorious. We have always been on a pathway of light, and we are on it even now.

At least, that's the way I see it.

What do you prefer?

Game on.

Illustrations

Energetic Definitions of Terms

5 Senses: term that designates the limitations of this BSC, also the name for the resulting manifested mind-body instrument.

Action: the instantaneous collision of (i) a desire or idea, (ii) the identification that it has not yet manifested on the 5 Senses Spectrum, (iii) activated beliefs that dictate acceptable expenditures of energy to address the lack.

Anger: the emotion of becoming.

Attention: the conscious perception of energies from all possible wavelengths of being.

Awakening: the conscious experience of expanding from a point of great limitation.

Belief: energetic structure that affects, modifies, and defines the perception of energy. A way of molding energy into experience.

Belief System Complex (BSC): a collection of interconnected energetic structures that affect the perceptions of energy.

Change: the conscious perception of new energy.

Consciousness: the capacity to perceive energetic wavelengths; the awareness of what can energetically be perceived.

Contrast: a difference between frequencies.

Control: the reduction of energies into the accepted framework of possibilities of the BSC.

Core Frequency: a being's unique energetic frequency in all of creation.

Dimension: the experience of a composite of wavelengths.

Effortlessness: the momentary cessation of participation in beliefs about body or action, in the 5 Senses BSC.

Fear: the emotion of furthest limitation.

Focus: the sensation of the narrowing of the perception of energies to align with the current capacity of the mind.

Frequency: place of understanding.

Hierarchy: a manifestation of 5 Senses beliefs.

Inspiration: the perception of more expansive frequencies that indicate energetic direction.

Intuition: the perception of frequencies that have not yet been molded by the 5 Senses BSC.

Joy: the emotion of right judgment.

Manifestation: energy that has been filtered and molded by way of beliefs.

Mass Consciousness: resonance with the composite of frequencies called the Physical Dimension.

Memory: a manifestation of the expansion of conscious perception to more than one frequency.

Mind: the conscious embodiment of the frequency of limitation with which you resonate for this experience. The name you have given your consciousness in the 5 Senses BSC.

Miracle: a low- to no-possibility outcome based upon the summation of conscious and unconscious beliefs in the BSC.

Momentum: the conscious embodiment of energization of a frequency.

Physical Dimension: the composite of frequencies with which humanity, The Chorus, and many other beings resonate.

Possibility: the conscious perception of the simultaneous existence of two opposing beliefs within the 5 Senses BSC, the conscious perception of choice.

Reality: how energy is perceived. The current perception of energy by way of the 5 Senses BSC.

Time: the underlying, unconscious constructs through which energy is molded before it manifests. An agreement of the 5 Senses BSC, as are Body and Distance.

Transcendence: expansion to the perception of more frequencies.

Trust: the momentary cessation of participation in beliefs about time.

Acknowledgments

I know that The Chorus might suggest you don't need to thank nonphysical beings for their infinite love, but it feels like the right place to start. Thank you – all of you – for standing by me through the hard times, for your patience and humor as we worked together, and for reminding me to celebrate even my most human moments. (I could've gone without the 4 a.m. wake-ups to write this thing, but I can give you feedback later.)

Thank you, Maggie McReynolds and Sky Kier of Un-Settling Books, for being not just talented editors, but incredible stewards of this process. Your openness, heartfelt advice, and encouragement have left an indelible mark on me. As has Kirby, blanket monster.

Thank you, also, to all the incredible writers of Un-Settling Books – you made me feel welcomed and understood in a way I didn't know was possible. When you can show up rumpled, mystified, sluggish, or slap-happy and are still well received, you know you've found a special group of people.

Thank you, Inez, my dear friend. You've seen the highs, the lows, and a fair amount sh*t that neither of us could understand at the time (and, let's be honest, we'll be the first to admit that we probably still don't understand it). And yet through it all you never let it undo your hope of what this could become. You showed me what faith looks like.

Stacy, your incredible courage kept the light burning when I was all but extinguished. You held a space for me to understand all of this, particularly when the world outside had no place for it. If we can all hold space for each other with as much love, radiance, and style as you have, then truly remarkable things are ahead.

Kyle, no matter how many voices showed up, you never let me forget my own. No matter how many dazzling things were revealed, your focus never wavered from my well-being. There is no way to measure a strength like yours. People may marvel at my journey, but I know that we did this together. Thank you. For everything.

And to my little one, my dear heart, the best memories of mornings spent writing this book are the ones when you would crawl into my lap and disrupt the writing. I love you more than words can express. Now clean up your Legos.

About the Author

Prior to The Chorus, I spent nearly two decades working as a Data and Technology Strategist, typically in start-up environments. Essentially my job was to help figure out worthwhile things to do with large datasets or unusual tech. I loved it. Then my health started to deteriorate, The Chorus showed up, and, well, you know the rest. Presently, I reside in the beautiful state of Colorado with my family. To follow along with what The Chorus and I are up to, visit www.KatieandTheChorus.com.

Where to Go from Here

Thank you for reading our book!

Would you like to hear recordings of me channeling The Chorus? Or listen to longer discussions on what they are sharing? Then check out our podcast, *Our Next Existence.*

In each episode I channel a message from The Chorus, then discuss the meaning in the human context. Episodes are about one hour long. Season One corresponds to this book, discussing similar and some adjacent topics. It is structured like a class, where each episode builds on the next. You can start at the beginning or jump to an episode with a topic that interests you.

For example, on the topic of trust, you might want to check out:

- S01E05 Beliefs in Trust & the Origins of Karma
- S01E22 Human Mutants, Anxiety Disorders, & How Trust Brings Us into the Present Moment

Related to human mental health, see:

- S01E03 The Energetic Definition of Mind & Also You're Not Crazy
- S01E07 How Humans Learn & Why Positive Thinking Can Be Hard to Do
- S01E12 Prevention, Protection, Love, & Only Expansive Humans Experience Depression
- S01E14 Human Energetic Perception, Conspiracy Theories, and What Underlies Humanity's Current "Mental Instability"

View a current list of Season 1 Episodes at
www.KatieandTheChorus.com/Podcast

Each episode page on our website features a web player and episode transcript so you can listen or read on the site. The podcast is also available on Apple, Google, Spotify, Amazon, JioSaavn, and many other providers.

To receive updates about the podcast and future books, as well as new messages from The Chorus, sign up for our newsletter at www.KatieandTheChorus.com/Newsletter.

Finally, if you liked our book, the best way to support it would be by recommending it to friends or leaving a review on Amazon. This book is self-published, and Amazon reviews really help books like ours to appear when people search for related topics, as well as help them to decide if it's a good fit. Thank you!

If you have any questions, please don't hesitate to email us at: Team@KatieandTheChorus.com.

We love you, infinitely.

Printed in the USA
CPSIA information can be obtained
at www.ICGtesting.com
CBHW062344271223
3004CB00007B/497

9 798985 257618